RAISED BED GARDENING FOR BEGINNERS

BUILD YOUR OWN RAISED BED GARDEN IN 5 SIMPLE
STEPS TO GROW DELICIOUS FRUITS & VEGETABLES

FREDERICK WHEATLY

CONTENTS

INTRODUCTION

Gardening is highly complicated. At least, this is what a lot of people think. Many people believe that to be a good gardener, you must be born with the skill. This is where the myth of having a green thumb comes in. It just seems like some people have a knack for gardening and can grow beautiful and lush plants, while others seem to kill even the simplest of plants.

While it is true that some people are more naturally talented when it comes to gardening, you can still develop the skill and become a fantastic gardener even if you have never done it before. The truth is that gardening is a skill that needs to be developed, and you need to know what the correct practices are before you begin doing anything. If you follow a few simple principles, then you will be able to grow a beautiful and lush garden in no time. Gardening is a hobby people love and enjoy because it is so rewarding. If you can put in the work at the beginning, you can reap the rewards in a very tangible way.

There are many different types of gardening out there. The type of gardening that will be focused on in this book is raised bed gardening. This is entirely different from any other gardening type because you must first build a structure before you can grow your garden. A raised bed garden simply lifts the garden bed above the natural ground level. This aspect is hugely beneficial when you do not have a lot of garden space or do not have natural soil to start planting. And also, in many people's opinion, it looks a whole lot better than just randomly planting things on the natural ground. You have much more control over how big your plants get, where they spread, and how everything looks.

Not everybody lives on a large plot of land where you can grow things on the natural ground. Many people live in townhouses or apartments. Just because you do not have ample outdoor space does not mean that you do not deserve to have a beautiful garden that produces fruit and vegetables. It is an enriching experience when you're able to enjoy food from the work of your own hands. It is an experience that I believe everybody should have regardless of the type of home they live in or how big their yard is.

There has been a rise in the number of people interested in gardening and growing their own fruits and vegetables. When you grow your own fruits and vegetables, you can be sure that there are no pesticides and everything is entirely organic. The fruits and vegetables you produce will be much healthier than those you can commercially buy in the store. While there may not be anything inherently wrong with store-bought fruit and vegetables, there is something different about the ones you grow by yourself. Once you taste your own fruit and vegetables, you will definitely see the difference in flavor as well as color and vibrance.

You'll be more motivated to make delicious recipes that you and your family look forward to eating. Gardening is also a great way to get your family and children involved in food-making. It becomes a learning process that everybody can get excited about. When the food is ready to be eaten, children get a lot more excited about eating their vegetables because they had a part to play in growing them. I have also included some really delicious and simple recipes you can make with your own fruits and vegetables. These recipes are incredibly quick and easy, but they beautifully showcase your vegetables. I hope it serves as some inspiration on what to do with the produce that you have successfully grown. It gives you a goal to work towards at the end of the growing season.

This book will also teach you everything you need to know about building your raised bed garden. It can seem incredibly daunting to start building something from scratch, but if you have the right direction, then it will not be so hard. Once you know how, using my five simple step guide, you can put together a raised bed garden relatively quickly. This book will take you through every aspect of building and caring for a raised bed garden. If you have any questions about what materials you should use or what kind of raised bed garden you should build, then you will find the answers in the pages of this book.

Once you have your raised bed garden up and running, you will need some guidance on how to start growing plants in a healthy way. Don't worry, I'm not going to leave you hanging because you will find that information in this book as well. Everything that you need to know about how to make your soil healthy, grow healthy plants, keep away pests, diseases, and anything in between will be covered in this book. By the time you reach the end, you will have all the information you need to sustain a healthy and beautiful garden. It will not be something you can do just this year but for every year to come. Gardening is a long-term skill; if you do it right, you can have a healthy garden year upon year. For most gardeners, this is the ultimate goal and is one that you can definitely reach.

The answers will be here for you no matter what your questions are or what you need guidance on along the journey to building a healthy and sustainable raised bed garden. We will start from the beginning to ensure that you can build a healthy raised bed structure and then move on to the actual planting and gardening. This will help you get a complete picture of what you need to do before you get started. It is advisable to read the whole book before you start taking action. Then you can go back to the relevant sections as you begin implementing the steps. So without any further introduction, let's dive into Chapter 1.

1

WHY RAISED BED GARDENING?

There are many reasons you should choose raised bed gardening over regular gardening. You will be able to control the health of the soil in which you are growing your plants. This allows you to grow much healthier plants that live longer and produce much higher quality fruit and vegetables.

Many people are confused about what a raised bed garden actually is. In simplest terms, a raised bed garden is a contained bed of soil above the level of the rest of the garden. When the garden is elevated, you are able to monitor it a lot better. You can have the plants at eye level so that you can see what's going on without being in the garden. When your garden is growing in a contained facility, it gives you a better ability to get in there and work on your garden. You can do this without impacting the overall shape because you have parameters in which you can work on it.

Many people live in areas where their soil is an issue. Some challenges could be your home being surrounded by concrete, living in an area that has a lot of clay, or living in an area that is full of dry and fine sand. All of these scenarios mean that it's going to be really difficult for you to grow a healthy garden. Simply raising your garden above the level of the natural soil in your area will allow you to have better control over your garden and allow you to grow it healthily and the way you want to. You won't necessarily be limited to what is available to you in your garden. Your plant roots do not have to reach the contaminated or inhospitable soil below.

There are lots of things that you are going to have to consider when starting a raised bed garden. The first thing is that you have to know all the pros and cons to this type of gardening so that you can make better decisions and know whether it's a good fit with your desired garden plan.

PROS OF RAISED BED GARDENING

There are many positives to building a raised bed gardening system. If you are on the fence about creating a raised bed garden, then it's good to understand the benefits. It gives you a better idea of what a raised bed garden can provide so that you are better equipped to deal with it. It also gives you a better idea of what to expect from your raised bed garden.

Better Drainage

One of the most important benefits of a raised bed garden is the fact that it provides you with better drainage for your plants. Most gardening novices believe that the more water, the better. However, there is a limit to the amount of water your plants should have access to. Simply overwatering your plants could cause them to die out. This is why drainage is essential to your gardening system. Sometimes you are unable to control the amount of water that gets into your garden. This is particularly so if you live in a rainy climate or in a season where you get a lot of rain. Having a proper drainage system will prevent any molding and flooding of your garden.

You might also be in an environment where your soil is not conducive to draining. Good soil will soak up the water so that the water does not stand in your garden. However, if your soil type is heavy, such as soil that has a lot of clay in it, there will not be a lot of drainage happening. Raising your garden above the soil level will allow you to prevent the negative impacts of having this kind of soil in your area. You are not going to be limited by the soil in your yard.

Higher Yields

A raised bed garden will bring a higher yield of plant growth. A higher yield just means that you will be able to get more fruits and vegetables from your plants. The reason this happens in a raised bed garden is that there is better root growth from the improved soil quality in your raised bed garden. You will also notice that ornamental plants are a lot more lush and beautiful.

A raised bed garden also allows you to contain your garden in a smaller area while maintaining the quality of the plants. You are able to grow a lot more plants in a smaller space. This is incredibly beneficial for those who have smaller yards to work with. Most people are scared to start growing a garden because they believe they do not have the space to do so. A raised bed garden allows you to work with what you have and still create a beautiful and thriving garden.

Expanded Growing Season

Plants grow in seasons. This means that there will be seasons when your garden is going to be a lot drier, and your plants will die. Then, in other seasons, your plants will thrive and grow a lot faster and be much healthier. Typically, in the spring and summer months, your garden will be lush and beautiful. In the fall and winter months, your garden will start to die out. This has nothing to do with you or how you are taking care of your garden. We see this type of growing and dying cycle take place in all-natural plants, with the exception of evergreens.

When you have a raised bed garden, you have a higher likelihood of stretching out the growing season of your plants. The better drainage in your soil will speed up the soil warming, allowing you to start planting earlier in spring. Your plants will be able to start growing before the typical growing season starts. In the wet seasons, your soil will be able to dry out a lot faster, and this allows planting to continue between rains.

Maintenance (Your Back Will Thank You)

If you have been gardening the traditional way, then you know a lot of bending is involved. You have to bend in order to weed, water, and generally maintain the plants, which can be uncomfortable. This is especially so when the garden is still in the early phases.

Using Difficult Sites

Not every kind of terrain will be conducive to growing a garden. This fact has stopped many people from being able to create and grow a healthy garden. With raised bed gardening, you can grow a garden any way you like. Since the garden is raised above the natural terrain, you could theoretically grow your garden wherever you'd like. For example, you could create a raised bed garden on a rooftop terrace that is made from solid concrete. It doesn't take a gardening expert to realize that you cannot grow a healthy garden on a concrete surface. However, since a raised bed garden is lifted above the natural terrain, you would be able to sustain and grow an amazing garden in this situation.

CONS OF RAISED BED GARDENING

While there are many positives to a raised bed garden, it is also important to note that there are a few cons. When you know what these drawbacks are, you'll be better prepared to deal with them and anticipate parts you may struggle with. Understanding the concept as a whole will allow you to create a more sustainable plan for your raised bed garden.

The Raised Soil Is More Exposed to Heat and Cold Than Surface Soil

When you create a raised bed garden, you are lifting the soil above the natural layer of the surface soil. This means that the raised layer of soil might be more susceptible and exposed to heat and cold. This is especially so if you live in an area with very extreme conditions. If you live in a place where there are moderate temperatures all year round, then you're probably not going to have to concern yourself with this kind of problem.

The good news is that there are things that you can do to help mitigate this issue. In most cases, your plants will be affected by extreme heat and cold when the sidewalls of your raised beds are not thick enough. All you have to do is ensure that you use the right thickness and type of material to prevent the extreme temperatures from reaching the soil. In later chapters, we will discuss what materials should be used when creating a raised bed garden.

Raised Soil Can Dry Out More Quickly Than Surface Soil

When soil is raised above the natural level, it is more susceptible to drying out. Water retention is something you must consider when you have a raised bed garden. This is a very fixable problem, so it is nothing to be too concerned about. However, you must be conscious of it and ensure that you are watering your garden enough.

Raised Beds Require Space Between the Beds for Movement

When creating a raised bed garden, you will be building many different raised beds for the different plants that you will be growing. You will need to create space in between each one of your raised beds so that you have room to walk through. In a regular garden, you would not need to do this because you would be able to walk through the different areas of your garden. In a raised bed garden, you cannot walk on top of the raised bed.

This is something to think about if you have a small space to work with. You will be losing some of your gardening space to create walking space. This might be a dealbreaker if you have a tiny yard to work with. It is something to think about before creating your raised bed garden.

The Permanence of Containerized Raised Beds

Depending on your situation, this can be thought of as a positive or a negative. The actual raised bed is going to be a pretty permanent structure in your yard. If you need to relocate your garden, then it means that you'll have to deconstruct and then reconstruct in the new area. This can be a lot of work, and it is something to think about if you are planning on moving in the coming years. However, if you are planning on planting a garden, then chances are you are thinking of doing so on a permanent basis.

DIFFERENT TYPES OF RAISED BEDS

There are two types of raised beds that you can choose to make. They each have their advantages and disadvantages. It is something to think about when you are considering creating a raised bed garden.

Temporary Raised Ground Bed

The first type is a temporary raised bed. As the name suggests, this is just a temporary raised bed that you can use to grow your plants. What you have to do for this is add a few inches of soil to your ground-level garden. That is not a lot of work, and many people choose to do this because of its simplicity. It is also much cheaper because you do not have to construct a framework for the soil and the raised bed.

The negative side to this is the fact that it is only temporary. If you want to continue growing your garden throughout the years, you'll have to reconstruct this every year. There are no walls built to contain the soil, and this might mean that erosion will take place on the top of the bed. A lot of the soil can wash away onto walkways as well as over hillsides and other areas. This means that you will be losing a lot of your healthy soil as well as creating a certain type of pollution by letting the fertilizer get into areas where it could be harmful.

Permanent Containerized Raised Beds

In most cases, a permanent raised bed is the most beneficial type of raised bed garden. If you are thinking about creating a raised bed garden and putting in the work for it, this is the best option. Since it will be a permanent structure, you do not have to worry about recreating it every year. Your plants, as well as your soil, will be safe within the confines of your raised bed. You will be creating walls to keep everything in as well as keep everything secure. If you live in an area susceptible to extreme weather, then a permanent structure made with the right materials can help protect your garden from the elements.

On the negative side, a permanent raised bed garden does mean that you are going to have to put in a lot more work, and it will cost more money to get started. Noise and traffic barriers might be created in your area while you are constructing your raised bed. It is a good idea to speak with your neighbors and let them know that there will be slight disruptions while you build it. This will prevent any complaints or angry neighbors throughout the process. Once the raised bed has been built, this will no longer be a problem.

2

PLANNING AND PREPARING FOR YOUR GARDEN

C reating a raised bed gardening system will take some planning and preparation. If you plan and prepare correctly, the rest of the process will be much easier, and you can be sure that your raised bed garden will be structurally sound. Nobody can build something sustainable that will last for a long time if they have not appropriately planned for it.

PICKING THE RIGHT SPOT

The first thing you'll need to do to plan for your raised bed garden is to think about where you want to place it. You will need to look at the space you have available so that you can choose one that's going to work for you and your garden. The location of your raised bed garden will need to consider a few crucial variables. These are the sun and shade, airflow, drainage, and accessibility. Choosing the right location will make the rest of the process a lot easier. It's important to remember that once your raised bed garden is built, it's a permanent structure, so it is vital to ensure you select the most optimal position to place your raised bed before you begin building.

Let's talk about the sun and shade first. We all know plants need a certain amount of sunlight in order to grow and produce optimum yields. This is especially so when it comes to fruit and vegetables. If you want to encourage high growth rates and yields, you need to ensure enough sun is reaching your garden. This means that you should choose a space that is quite open and is not going to be overshadowed by walls, trees, and other obstacles. It is a good idea to look at where the sun hits your yard or gardening space. Make some observations throughout the day; the sun's movement can cause shade in areas closer to the evening where there wasn't any shade in the morning. If you live in a colder climate, then it is especially important for the plants to get as much sunlight as possible. If you live in a hotter climate, you might need to provide some shade in the summer months to help your crops handle the heat. A simple shade cloth will do the trick. If you are considering using a shady spot in your yard, then you should reserve this for plants that thrive under shady conditions. Some of these are leafy green vegetables, chives, and currant bushes.

The airflow in the area is the next variable you need to consider when it comes to where you will build your raised bed garden. If there is too much exposed area around your garden, then this could make them susceptible to high winds and turbulence. This means that your plants could be placed in a position where they could be destroyed or damaged by these heavy winds. If you choose an area with a lot of sunlight, there is a high chance that it will be in an exposed area. If this is the case, it is wise to offer some sort of shelter to your garden. This could be in the form of a solid wall or a fence. This will break the winds and make it so that they are not as harsh on your garden. With this being said, these types of solid walls and fences can cause the wind to form destructive eddies, so if you decide to build a solid wall or fence, make sure that it's not too close to your garden. The best protectors from heavy winds are hedges, semipermeable structures, or woven and open fences. These allow some of the wind to come through but will filter it instead of deflecting it. Good airflow is essential to the health of your garden. It keeps fungal diseases away and can make it less appealing to various insects and pests. This is why you shouldn't completely protect your garden from all types of wind and airflow.

Drainage is also important because you need a good amount of moisture in your soil but not so much that your plants start to rot. Having thick walls and fences can block the soil from the rain, leaving the soil too dry. If your garden is right under an overhanging tree, then the tree could soak up most of the rainwater and reduce what is available to your crops. Since your garden is going to be a raised bed garden, you will probably not have to worry about it being at a sunken level. If a garden is sunken, then this could cause water to stand for too long and cause plants to be overwatered and start to rot. In the dry seasons, you would have to water your plants to ensure they stay hydrated.

The final thing you would have to consider when picking the right spot for your garden is accessibility. You want to choose a spot that is easy for you to get to and work in. This means that there shouldn't be too many obstructions in the area, and it should be cleared away of anything that could make it harder to work on your garden. It is a good idea to have a designated area to build your raised bed so you can do everything in a concentrated area. If you plant multiple raised beds all over the lawn, it could be challenging to move from one place to another as you check your plants. Chances are, you will need to check on your garden every few days, so you need to make sure that it's going to be easy for you to do so. This might not seem like such a big deal now, but as time goes on and you continue caring for your garden, it can be pretty annoying to walk all over the place to tend to your garden. This is especially so if you have a large piece of property.

It is very important to analyze the space you have for your garden. Make sure you understand the pros and cons of each spot. This will allow you to make an informed decision of where you want to build your raised bed garden. You must do this before you start preparing to start building. It is tough to make changes once you've started and even more so once you have created the structure. If you have done your research and taken the time to think about the area in which you want to build a raised bed, then you can be confident in moving on to the next stage of your raised bed gardening journey.

CONSIDER THE SIZE

Once you have identified the perfect spot for your raised bed garden, you need to consider the size you want it to be. This is incredibly important for more than just aesthetic reasons. You need to have the right size so that you can easily take care of your garden. If it is too wide, then you will not be able to tend to the garden well enough. You need to be able to reach across your garden to prune, weed, and monitor it. Remember, you will not be able to hop into your raised bed to do the gardening. Most raised beds are about three to four feet wide, but make sure you are comfortable with the size before you commit to building.

Height is also something that needs to be considered when it comes to the size of the raised bed garden. If you are placing your raised bed on a hard surface, like concrete or clay soil, you will need to ensure that the raised bed is tall enough for the plants to have deep roots. This is especially so if you are planting root vegetables. At least 10 to 12 inches is a good depth. It would be best if you also thought about height accessibility. If you know that you will have problems bending down for long periods, you should consider building a raised bed that is relatively high. It should not be too tall otherwise, you will have trouble tending to the garden. You still need to be able to reach over to the other side of the raised bed, so make sure you take all of this into consideration when you are planning the size of your raised bed garden.

WHAT ABOUT IRRIGATION?

Irrigation is essential to the health and growth of your garden. It is the process of feeding water to your crops in an artificial manner. This helps to fulfill all of your plants' water needs. You can also give your garden nutrients through irrigation if they are not getting enough from the site. You could use pipes, sprinklers, drips, and many other irrigation methods. What you use will depend on you and the needs you have in your garden.

In most cases, a drip irrigation system will work best for a raised bed garden. All you need to do is attach a hose to a tap and run it through the garden. If you choose this method and many other methods of irrigation, then you should ensure that your raised bed garden is close to a tap or water source. If not, try and ensure that you can feed a hose pipe to the area in a manner that's not going to get in the way of the rest of your yard.

Once you have your garden all set up, you need to set up an irrigation system. This will ensure that you are getting your plants enough moisture to grow healthy. One of the most effective irrigation systems is a drip irrigation system. It is also not too difficult to set up, so it is a good option. All you need is a network of pipes and drip emitters attached to these pipes. These drip emitters are specifically designed to release water at a very slow pace. This eliminates water waste and prevents overwatering.

If you plan it properly, installing the drip irrigation system will not take you more than a couple of hours. The first thing that you're going to want to do is to plan out your garden. You need to know where you want the pipe to run from and attach it to a water source, like a tap. Having a plan will allow you to decide how long you need your pipes to be and how many drip emitters you will need. Your pipe will need to snake around the trees, plants, and other obstacles in your garden in order to get to the raised beds. You can buy pre-punched or unperforated tubing, which will require you to punch your own holes so that you can attach the admitters to the tubing. If you have an unusual layout in your garden, then the unperforated tubing might be the better choice since you can customize the system as you would like. It is best to talk to someone who works in the garden store because they will be able to point you to what is available in your area and what will work best for your garden. You can also take a few pictures to show them so that you can get a better idea of what you need.

Once you have everything you need, you'll have to connect the pipe and water timer to the outside tap. Make sure you are screwing it tightly, so water does not drip from the source. The next thing that you are going to need to do is to set up the pipe system. The pipe might be very stiff when you first bring it home, so the best thing you can do is to unravel it and allow it to lay out in the sun for a few hours. This will soften the plastic and make it easier for you to maneuver.

When you are ready, you can start laying down the pipe.

After the pipe has been laid down to your liking, you can start securing it with ground stakes. These stakes are shaped like hooks with a sharp point on the other end. This allows the stake to grab hold of the pipe and stake it to the ground. If you have areas where the tubing has to turn at a sharp angle or needs to branch out to another section, then you'll need to use T or elbow connectors. All you will have to do is cut the end of the tubing and connect those pieces. Then you can continue laying down your pipe. Next is connecting the drippers. There are many different types of drippers that you could have. All of them will come with directions on the back of the pack, which is much easier to follow. There might be specific instructions that you need to follow for the type of dripper that you purchase. Follow the directions and push the drippers into the pipe, and then it is time to test your irrigation system. Turn on the water system and then walk around to see if you can find any leaky connectors or drippers that are not working correctly. You can also check whether your garden is receiving the amount of water that it needs. From here, you can adjust accordingly and fix what needs to be fixed.

The last thing that you'll need to do is to set your water timer. You will be changing the water timer throughout the seasons, depending on how much water is coming from rain. You will also need to research how much water your plants actually need. Some plants require far less water than others, so you need to be aware of each plant's water requirements so that you do not overwater them. You also need to avoid running your irrigation system for frequent short periods throughout the day. When you do this, all the water stays at the surface, and the roots will do the same. This means that your plants will dry out a lot quicker and will not be as strong since they do not have deep roots. As a rough guide, you should set your timer for twenty to thirty minutes, 3 to 4 times per week in the springtime, twenty to thirty minutes each day of the week in the summertime or dry months, and fifteen to twenty minutes, 2 to 3 times a week in the fall. In the winter, your plants will most likely dry out and die, so there might not be much reason to water them. This all depends on the type of plant and the climate you live in.

3

CONSTRUCTING YOUR
RAISED BED

N ow that you have got all the essential planning done for your raised bed garden, it is time to start thinking about constructing it. It can seem like an incredibly complicated process to build a functioning and sustainable raised bed garden, but it can also be really simple. You just have to make the right choices along the way because you want your raised bed garden to last for a long time.

The first thing you will need to do when you are planning to build a raised bed garden is to consider the various materials you can use. Many materials can be used to build a raised bed garden, each of which has pros and cons. Understanding these pros and cons is crucial so you can make an informed decision for yourself. You should consider three things when picking out materials for your garden: longevity, cost, and safety.

Longevity just means how durable the material is and whether it will stand the test of time. You do not want something that will wear down in a few years and that you will have to replace. Replacing these materials can be a lot of work, and you're not going to get your money's worth. It would help if you kept in mind that your raised bed garden is going to be exposed to the outdoor elements as well as be in contact with moisture all the time. If you choose a material that rusts or molds quickly, it will not stand the test of time. Concrete or metal beds will have the most longevity compared to wooden and lumber materials.

Cost is also important to consider. You don't want to blow your budget when making a raised bed garden, but you also need to ensure that you're not just choosing the cheapest option. The truth is that higher-quality material will cost you more. This is why it is important to look at long-term and short-term costs. If you are only concerned about the short-term cost, you will likely pick the cheapest material. However, the chances are that this material will deteriorate quickly, and you'll have to replace it. This is an additional cost that you'll have to factor in. If you were to pay more upfront for higher quality material, you would not have to replace or fix it as often. With that being said, you also have to think about your current living situation. If you are renting or in a temporary home, you might be better off choosing a lower quality material at a cheaper cost since you could be moving soon. Regardless of whether you are looking to put down a lot of money upfront or looking for a more affordable option, it is always best to shop around and compare prices. This will ensure you get the best deal for your materials and are not overspending.

The final thing that you should be considering is safety. I know you might think this is just a garden and what safety has to do with it, but this aspect should not be overlooked. When growing a garden, you need to consider the plants' health and safety; if you choose to grow consumable fruit and vegetables, this is even more important. Many people decide to up-cycle certain materials to make their raised bed garden. This alone is not a bad idea, you just have to be careful about which materials you are using and be sure that you know the history of it. For example, some people use Styrofoam coolers, but polystyrene is a suspected carcinogen. Another common material is used car tires, which contain many chemicals and minerals that can be toxic to humans. Something else people do is try to salvage painted or treated wood, but if you do not know the origin or the age of this material, then it could very well be contaminated with toxic chemicals. This can be damaging for your plants and your health.

We will go through the best materials you should be using for your raised bed garden, but before we do that, let's talk about the things you should avoid. Here is a list of materials that you should give a skip when building your raised bed garden:

- Reclaimed or recycled wood
- Treated lumber
- Styrofoam
- Car tires
- Railroad ties; these are often treated with creosote which can be dangerous for plants and humans.
- Random plastic products. You can use some plastic for your raised bed garden, although it's not the best material to use. If you do choose to

use plastic, make sure that it is food grade and BPA-free.

MATERIALS TO CONSIDER

You can use many materials to build a raised bed garden. Still, we will be talking about a few of the best materials below. It is always best to do your research, and you need to know what's going to be feasible and available to you in your area. It is also a good idea to chat with the suppliers and see what they think would be best to use for your raised bed garden. Remember, different materials have pros and cons, and the one you choose needs to be one that will work for your area and your needs.

Cedar or Redwood

If you choose a wooden material to build a raised bed, then you need to make sure that it is durable, resistant to moisture, will not rot, and is resistant to termites. Of all the options available to you, cedar and redwood will be the best choices. The cost of these woods will vary depending on your location. Some US states have much more affordable redwood and cedar options, while others are more expensive. It is worth it to do your research to find out the most affordable option near you.

Cedar and redwood are incredibly durable wooden materials. If you choose to use this, your raised garden will last about ten years or longer. These two materials fall under softwood lumber, and they have natural tannins, making them more durable than other softwood options. The tannins also repel termites and rot. If you choose either of these options, you should make sure that the wood comes from responsibly managed forests. These will have an FSC certification on them. If you are unsure, it's a good idea to speak to the supplier about how the wood has been sourced.

Metal

Metal is a material that has become popular in the raised bed garden space. More and more people are choosing to build their raised bed garden using this material. This is no surprise because these raised bed gardens look modern and sleek, not to mention that metal is incredibly durable. They do not rot over time and will not shrink or swell with the moisture. If you live in a moist environment, choosing a metal material such as galvanized steel is a great option.

One worry when using metal as your material of choice is that it will get too hot in the warmer months. However, this should not be a cause for too much concern since damp soil will be able to buffer out these temperature swings. You just have to ensure that your garden is sufficiently watered, and you should be perfectly fine. Another positive to using metal is that many metal-raised bed kits are out there. This makes things much easier because you will get everything in one kit along with all the instructions. Just look at your local garden supply store and see what they offer. You might be surprised at how easy it will be to get your hands on one of these kits. Just make sure that whatever metal you are using is galvanized so that it will not rust over time.

Concrete Pavers, Cinder Blocks, or Brick

The above materials are incredibly sturdy and last a long time. In fact, these materials do make your raised bed garden quite permanent. You will most likely need to adhere them together with concrete or mortar, creating a very heavy and permanent structure. This means that if you decide to go with this material, you'll have to be shown the design and also be sure that you're not going to move it around. Your flexibility is limited when you use these materials.

It is possible to create a raised bed with concrete, bricks, or cinder blocks without some sort of adhesive. If you choose to do this, you'll need to ensure that your garden is pretty shallow. The taller you go, the more unstable it will be. If you live in an area prone to heavy rains and unpredictable weather, then it is not a good idea to not use adhesive with this material.

The type of adhesive that you use is also really important. Some types of glue can be toxic, so make sure that you do your research and pick something safe. You also want to ensure that your adhesive has completely dried before adding the soil and seeds. The moisture from the soil will make it very difficult for the adhesive to dry, so it is better to be safe than sorry in this regard.

FIVE SIMPLE STEPS TO BUILD A RAISED BED

Building a raised bed garden can be easy, especially if you follow these five steps. We will be going through exactly how to make a 4 x 8 ft bed. However, if you want to build something bigger or smaller, you just have to increase or decrease the size of the planks you use. If you're using other materials besides the wooden planks, then it will be slightly different in terms of methodology. When you are building a metal raised bed, then you can get a kit. However, you will be following the same basic principles regardless of the material that you are using. This is what you will need to create your bed:

- Two 2 x 12 planks. Each plank needs to be 8 feet long.
- Two2 x 12 planks. Each plank needs to be 4 feet long.
- 12 x pieces of rebar, each measuring 2 feet long.
- A mallet
- Newspaper or cardboard
- Soil

Choose the area where you want to build a raised bed garden and ensure that it is entirely flat. You might have to take time to clear out some space for your garden or manually flatten the area. Please make sure you spend time thinking about where you want your raised bed to be so that it is convenient for you and easy to access.

Step 1: Plan It Out

Lay your planks flat on their sides so that the inner corners touch each other. You should see a rectangle made up of each plank's inner edges. The planks of the same size should be running parallel to each other.

Step 2: Start Building the Walls

Lift one of the longer boards onto its side, so it stands up. Hammer in two pieces of rebar one foot away from each corner.

Step 3: Complete building the walls

Prop up one of the shorter planks and use a piece of rebar at the center of these for temporary support. Then lift the longer plank and do the same as you did with the first long plank.

Step 4: Reinforcement

Next, you will need to reinforce the frame by hammering rebar a few inches deep into the ground and a foot from each corner of the short planks.

You can remove the temporary support. You can then add two pieces of rebar about 2 ft apart on the longer sides. This allows you to reinforce the frame to be ready to be filled with soil. Make sure you hammer in each piece of rebar until about 6 to 10 inches are left exposed on top of the ground.

Step 5: Prepare the Foundation

Take your newspaper and cardboard and lay them down at the bottom of the bed. Ensure all the grass or soil underneath the raised bed is completely covered. Wet the newspaper and cardboard thoroughly. Doing this will ensure a moist environment for your garden to flourish. Once that is done, you can fill it with soil until just a few inches of space is left at the top. Dampen the soil so that it is ready for the next step.

Plant Your Garden

Your raised bed garden should now be ready for planting. Before getting into this, we are going to be talking more about choosing your plants later. You will also need to decide whether you want to start growing your plants from seeds or use seedlings.

As you can see, it is pretty simple to set up a raised bed garden made from wooden planks. However, you can use this same method to make a raised bed out of any other material. You will not need to use rebar if you use heavier materials such as concrete blocks or bricks. All you will need to do is set up the bricks or blocks in the way you want them to be and adhere them together. Once the adhesive is dried, you can follow the steps with the newspaper or cardboard and then the soil. After this, you should be good to go.

KEEPING THE BIRDS OUT

Birds can be a real problem to any garden. Removing your garden from being disrupted by birds is completely optional. You have to decide whether or not it is going to be worth it for you. If you live in an area where the birds are not causing a problem, you don't have to worry about this. However, suppose you have noticed that birds are wreaking havoc on your garden or that it could be a potential problem. In that case, you should consider installing bird netting.

One of the best solutions to unwanted avian visitors is bird netting. This netting is designed to deter the birds from disturbing your garden, so it will not harm the birds in any way. They can be easily installed as all you need are the nets and the fixings. You will connect the nets to the fixings attached to your raised bed's ends. The net will cover the garden and provide protection. Since it is a net, it will still let sunlight through, so you do not have to worry about your plants getting less sunlight because of these nets.

4

GARDENING BASICS

Once your raised bed is constructed, it is time to start planting. Some people believe they have to have a green thumb to grow healthy plants. While it is true that some people do have a natural knack for gardening, it is certainly a skill that you can learn. If you put the right things into practice, then you'll be able to grow a healthy and thriving garden.

PICKING THE RIGHT SOIL

When you are growing fruits and vegetables, different soils are needed in order for them to grow healthy. Paying attention to the type of fruits and vegetables you are planting will help you choose the most suitable soil. This section will provide the expertise to ensure that your soil is well prepared for the fruit and vegetables you want to plant.

For Fruit

Getting the perfect soil to grow your fruit is a delicate balance. In most cases, fruit trees and bushes will grow best when the soil is well-drained with a sandy and loamy texture. If there are too many rocks or clay, it will make it very difficult for the plants to grow and flourish. It would be best if you also made sure that the soil has enough nutrients because this is the key to allowing the trees and bushes to grow tasty and delicious fruit.

You are free to use ready-made potting soil designed for fruit. However, it is usually best to have full control over what goes into your soil mixture. An equal proportion of peat, bark, and sand typically makes a pretty good home for your fruit plants. The soil needs to be capable of retaining a lot of moisture as well as being able to drain away any excess water. You should never use plain garden soil as it does not have enough drainage for your fruit trees. Suppose you are growing fruit that requires acidic conditions, for example, blueberries and cranberries. In that case, these must be grown in something called ericaceous compost. This simply means that the compost has a pH between four and five.

For Vegetables

Vegetables can flourish in a raised bed garden if you choose the right soil mix. Most vegetables are incredibly heavy feeders, so you must ensure that your soil is nutrient-rich. The more nutrients available to your vegetables, the more likely you are to get healthy and tasty food. A vegetable garden needs nutrient-rich soil with enough moisture, fertilizer, and regular care and attention. If you get everything else right but miss out on nutrient-rich soil, then it will be for nothing. This is why you need to focus on this first before you move on to the other aspects of growing a vegetable garden.

The most straightforward mix for your soil will be 50% compost and 50% topsoil. There are many people and gardeners who believe that using the local soil is a really good idea. This is because it considers the climate and the environment around you. When choosing compost, you need to go for something of good quality. The higher the compost quality, the more nutrients will be fed to your plants. You can choose to create your compost by decomposing organic matter, or you can purchase compost. It is important to note that composting by yourself will take a while, so you must prepare for this in advance.

Topsoil is what you will find in the first 3 to 6 inches of soil on top of the ground. If you do not have good-quality topsoil in your garden, you can purchase some topsoil from a gardening store. This topsoil is going to have a loamy texture, and it's going to be a mix of clay, sand, and silt. Buying topsoil from a gardening store or centre ensures there are very few clumps and debris. This can often be a lot better for your plants, depending on what your natural soil looks like.

SOIL IMPROVERS

At the end of the day, you need good quality soil if you want to grow any type of plant. When it comes to growing fruit and vegetables and consumable plants, you need to be sure that your soil is nutrient-dense. This will ensure that whatever food you are growing will taste delicious and be packed with nutrients. Once the plants have already started growing, it is pretty much too late to fix their nutrient properties. It is not your job to control the actual plant growth, but you can ensure that you are feeding the soil the right things so that the soil can, in turn, feed your plants.

If you have poor quality soil, then there's no need to panic. You can do things to improve the quality of your soil and, in turn, improve the quality of your plants. It will take some intentionality, and you will have to take some steps to get there. Still, you will be able to have good quality soil in the future.

Fertilizer

I'm sure you have heard about fertilizer before. A fertilizer is just referring to plant food. It is an extensive term that can either be a mixture of chemicals or a naturally occurring matter that is used for improving the health and growth of plants. Fertilizers come in many shapes and forms. You can get it in a liquid, water-soluble or granular form, or get it in the compost where the fertilizer is already mixed into the soil. There are also plenty of organic fertilizers that are available on the market, such as bone meal and chicken manure.

You can think of plants just like a growing baby. Just as a baby needs to be taken care of and fed nutritious food for it to grow, the same applies to plants. If you do not provide your plants with the right amount of nutrients, then you will not see them grow and be healthy. Fertilizers have been designed to give your plants exactly what they need. They are designed to provide the essential nutrients to your developing garden. You can think of it as a multivitamin or a meal replacement, but in the plant world. There are many fertilizers out there that improve the way the soil works. This means that it also helps the soil retain water and allows airflow throughout the soil. This is amazing for the plant's roots, so it's not just the flowering part of the plant that is benefiting from it.

Fertilizer is made up of many ingredients. Most of the popular fertilizers contain the essential elements for plant growth. These are nitrogen, potassium, and phosphorus. Nitrogen is vital to plant growth because it helps to increase the capacity to produce new flowers, fruit, and stems. You will find that adding nitrogen to your soil will increase the speed at which they grow. The quality of the plant and fruit, as well as the appearance for all, improve. Potassium helps to build up the protein in the plant. This is needed to allow the plant to fight off diseases. Potassium is also incredibly essential to photosynthesis, which we all know is the process in which plants turn light into food for themselves. The final nutrient is phosphorus, which helps the plants form strong root systems. It is also crucial in forming chlorophyll, which is incredibly important to photosynthesis. Phosphorus works hand-in-hand with potassium to keep the plant growing and healthy.

Maintenance

Maintenance is an incredibly important part of growing a healthy garden. It's not just planting the seeds and leaving them to their own devices. You have to be hands-on and take continuous care of the raised bed garden for it to grow and flourish. It is a commitment, but once you see your plants growing and thriving, you'll find it incredibly worthwhile.

Part of maintenance is adding compost to your garden. We have already spoken extensively about this topic, so we're not going to get into what is in the compost or how much you should be adding. Rather, it would be best if you consider adding compost to your garden in the fall season. Many people just prepare their garden for springtime; while this is incredibly important, you are missing out if you don't add compost in the fall as well. The compost will sit in the raised bed for the duration of winter, and it will not be completely broken down. You can cover the top with a few inches of mulch so that it can protect the compost throughout the winter. This will keep the nutrients inside the raised bed, and the soil will be better off during the growing season.

Another great thing to look into is soil amendments. As you continue working on the soil and grow your garden, you might notice that some things keep happening. Perhaps your soil seems to dry out quickly. In this case, there might be too much sand, which allows the water to evaporate and drain out quickly. You can correct this by adding organic matter or compost. This will thicken up the soil so that it can retain moisture. On the other hand, you might find that your soil is holding too much water, and it is standing. In this case, the opposite approach would be needed, and you can mix greensand fertilizer with the soil to loosen it up a bit.

There are plenty of different kinds of soil amendments out there, depending on what you are struggling with. It is essential to pay attention to your soil so that you can understand what the problems are. Once you know what the problems are, then you can find a solution for the specific issue. You can go to your gardening supply store and get some advice from them. Make sure that you explain exactly what is going on with your soil and what you are looking to resolve. It might also be a good idea to take a video or a picture of your soil so that you have some visual references to show them. Some amendments that might be recommended based on your specific problem are vermiculite, worm castings, greensand, cornmeal, straw meal, compost, or grass clippings.

Cover crops can also be a beneficial aspect of your garden to consider. They help to aerate the soil. This is especially so if you choose a cover crop that has a deep root system. An example of this is alfalfa. This deep root system will pull up the nutrients from the soil to the surface. This will make the nutrients readily available to your plants when it comes time to plant them. You can till the cover crop into the soil a few weeks before it comes time to plant.

Tilling is the process of mixing the soil by turning the first 6-10 inches of soil digging. This will help spread the nutrients around that the cover crop has produced. If your goal is to add more nitrogen to your soil, you should consider planting a few legumes as your cover crop. Fava beans and crimson clover are good examples of these. You can also add cover crops in the winter season when you are not growing anything. This will help maintain the soil's quality while nothing is growing.

A fundamental form of maintenance is called pruning. It is a form of preventive maintenance that can be used on both old and young plants. When you have a regular pruning schedule, you are protecting the plants and property from injury, damage, and pests. Pruning is where you remove the dead and sick branches, leaves, and stems. This allows room for brand new growth in the plants. It also reduces the risk of large branches falling and causing obstructions in your garden and on the garden floor. Pruning also helps to deter animals and pests from infesting your garden.

There are many different types of pruning. These include topping, thinning, raising, and reduction. Each has a different purpose, so you need to consider which will be best for your plant and situation. Topping is when you remove most of the branches all the way down to the trunk. This is usually used when people are trying to train a young tree to grow a certain way. Thinning is just removing a branch from the point where it connects to the main stem. This enhances light penetration so that the plant can gain more nutrients and helps you manage the growth. Raising is when you trim off the low-hanging points of the plant. When it's a large tree, this is usually done so that people and cars can walk underneath it. When it is a smaller plant, then you can do this so that you can have access to the soil and the plants that are lower to the ground. And finally, reduction is when you simply trim the volume off the plant. This can be for many reasons, including the fact that it is just getting too big.

Pruning is a skill that you will have to build up over time. Many people make the mistake of over-pruning. You shouldn't go wild and just start chopping things off. The best type of pruning for a raised bed garden is thinning. All you're doing is looking for the dead and dying pieces of your plant and chopping them off. It will allow more light to penetrate the plant and start to grow a lot better. When you first start out with pruning, it is usually better to take the conservative approach. Please don't go overboard; otherwise, you might regret it later.

Another way to maintain your garden is to provide your plants with a stake or some form of support.

When plants are young, the stems can be quite weak. This means that if there are heavy winds or an accident were to occur, the chances of the stems breaking are pretty high. If you give the plants some support, they will have a better chance of growing strong. Many people use stakes for growing vine plants, like tomatoes, but you can use them for any younger plant. All you have to do is hammer a stake into the ground and tie up the central stalk to it. Make sure the stake is placed extremely close to the main stalk, so you are not bending it over. You also don't want to hammer the stake too deeply into the ground, otherwise, you might cause trauma to the roots. As the plants grow, you might have to increase the size of the stakes. This is why it's important to have a look at your plants regularly so that you can see how they are growing and what their needs are.

Watering Your Plants

Anyone who has had a garden before knows they have to water it. This is a critical aspect of caring for your plants. It is also really important that you water them so that you can improve your soil quality. Anybody can just dump water onto their plants. Still, it takes experience to understand how the plants use the water. When you know how plants take up water, then you can give them the water they need in the most efficient way.

The roots' tips are responsible for the uptake and absorption of water in the soil. There are little root hairs on each one of these roots, and they aid in this process. If water only stays at the top layer of soil, then there will not be much water absorption at the roots. Many plants dig their roots very deep into the ground. This means you need to pour enough water onto your soil so it sinks deep into the ground. If you do not do this, then all you are doing is dampening the top layer of soil, which is not providing much benefit to your plants.

One of the biggest mistakes people make when watering their plants is that they just throw the water on them. They pour from a high point, meaning the water falls onto the leaves of the plant before it gets into the soil. The leaves of the plant do not need water. It is the soil that needs to soak up the water in order to feed it to the roots. You are wasting water and could damage your plant leaves if you pour water on top of them. This is especially so when plants are still young. These plants are very fragile, and if you pour water on them, there's a very high chance of them being damaged and breaking. It is best to focus the water at the soil level. If you have an irrigation system, then this is already happening for you. The water is dripped onto the soil and not poured onto the plant leaves.

It might seem like rocket science to think about when you should be watering your plants, but it is actually very easy. The first thing that you have to do is check the soil before you water it. Take your hand and push down on the soil to see if it is damp. It is not a big deal if the top of the soil is dry. In fact, this is pretty normal. Take your finger and dig it into the soil so that it is a few inches deep. If you find that the soil is still dry at this point, then it is time to water your plants. If there is moisture below the surface, then you can wait a day before you start watering.

The best time to water your plants is in the morning so that any excess water that has landed on the plant leaves can dry out. Too much water can cause your plant leaves and stems to rot. Sometimes it is challenging not to get any water on your plant leaves. If you water your plants in the morning, then the sun will dry out the extra water, and you don't have to worry about your plants getting diseased. It is definitely more difficult for diseases to grab a foothold on your plants when they are dry. It is not a huge catastrophe to water your plants in the evening but just be sure that you are more careful. Another benefit to watering your plants early in the morning is that the sun is not out in full force. This will prevent any unnecessary evaporation. The water has a chance to sink deep into the roots before the sun comes out to dry everything up.

It is also a good idea to cover the top layer of your soil with a thin layer of mulch. Mulch can be anything from shredded leaves, bark, hay or pine needles. These things will prevent excess evaporation from taking place. It protects the surface of your soil and ensures that your plants have the highest possibility of soaking up as much water and nutrients as possible. Just make sure that your mulch layer is not too thick. Just about an inch is perfect. If you make it too thick, this can have a counterproductive effect. It will prevent the water from getting down into the roots of your garden.

PESTS AND DISEASE

Pests and diseases are something that you are going to have to deal with if you have a garden. It can be so disheartening to put all your time and effort into your garden and then realize that it's been destroyed by unwanted guests. The good news is that there are things that you can do to prevent these pests and diseases. If they have already taken hold of your plants, then there are also things that you can do to get rid of them.

Common Pests

It is a really good idea to be prepared for any common pests that might want to attach themselves to your plants. One of the most common pests is called aphids. This is a broad term that encompasses quite a few flies. These can be black fly, green fly, and white fly. These aphids feed on the sap of your plants. They tend to infest the tips of new shoots, flower buds, and young plant leaves. Many of these insects can carry diseases and viruses which can transfer into your plant when they start to feed. Many of these viruses can make your plants sick and weak to a point where it stops the growth and leaves begin to fall off. There are many natural enemies to the aphid. These are hoverfly larvae and ladybirds. If you attract these insects to your garden, then nature can battle it out.

Another common pest is the caterpillar. While children love to watch these creatures wiggle around in the garden, they are not your plants' best friends. They can turn into beautiful butterflies, which we all love to see in our gardens, but they can also decimate a large portion of your crops. Caterpillars typically feed on specific types of crops. Peas and cabbage tend to be at risk of this. If you are growing these types of vegetables, you need to be more aware of caterpillars in your garden. You can inspect your leaves to see if you can find any caterpillars and then pick them off. If you want to use biological control, you can use a pathogenic nematode. This will infect the caterpillars with a disease, and they will die off.

Slugs and snails are abundant in a well-watered garden, and you can expect to see quite a few of these. Slugs are active regardless of the weather and will be out throughout the year, while snails are dormant in the colder months. Your plants can tolerate mild damage from these mollusks, but you do want to protect your most delicate plants. You can cover these with physical barriers such as cloches. You could also bring more wildlife to your garden, such as toads and hedgehogs.

Weevils are another pest that you might have to deal with. The larvae will feed on the root of your plants, and this is especially so when it comes to plants that are in pots or containers, so you need to be wary with your raised bed garden. The symptoms of weevils on the roots of your plants are similar to under-watering your plants. You'll notice things start to wither away because the roots can no longer take up water effectively. Once they have matured into adulthood, they will begin to feed on the leaves and foliage of the plants. You will notice that there is notching on the leaves' ends; this is how you know that weevils have been there. The natural enemies of the weevils are birds, frogs, and toads. This can really help bring down the population of these if you are struggling. You could also use biological control in the form of nematodes.

And the last pest that we are going to be talking about is rabbits. These are not insects, so you will have to take a different approach to deal with them. Most people love rabbits, and they are very cute. The problem comes in when they start chomping on all of your fruits and vegetables. A rabbit will feed on a large variety of your plants. They have an affinity for new shoots, which can be grazed down to the ground level. The best way to protect your plants is to enclose them. Since you have a raised bed garden, this might be enough. It all depends on how high the walls are for your raised bed. If the rabbits are still getting in there, then you need to cover up your young plants with a cloche or something similar to protect it.

How to Prevent Pests and Deal With Them

Now that you know the types of pests you will be dealing with, you need a plan to prevent them from getting to your plants and how to deal with them effectively. We have already spoken about a few ways in which you can deal with certain pests, but it is good to have a well-rounded strategy. There are plenty of things that you can do to help prevent problems from getting into your plants in the first place. Prevention will always be better than cure, but some things can be done once you are already dealing with pests.

The first thing you will want to do is ensure that your soil is healthy. Healthy soil will provide the nutrients your plants need to build healthy immune systems. This means they will be able to fight off any diseases and pests that do attack. The next thing you want to think about is the type of plants you will have in your garden. Some are more naturally pest-resistant than others. Choosing these kinds of plants will make it a lot easier on you when you have to deal with pests and diseases. You can also choose to plant certain more pest-resistant plants so they can chase away some of the pests you will be dealing with. Lemon grass, mint, and rosemary are all great options.

You also want to ensure that you are planting in the right place. Make sure that you understand your plants.

Certain plants are going to need more water, and others are going to need less. Some will need a lot of sunlight, and others can deal with more shade. If you plant them in the right place for their needs, you will have a higher chance of them being resistant to diseases and pests.

There are also plenty of beneficial insects out there that you can attract to your garden to help keep down the population of nasty insects. You want to do your best to attract these kinds of insects to your garden so that they can eat up the pests. Coriander, sweet asylum, sunflowers, and yarrow are all great ones to attract suitable types of insects. You can also repel the pests using strongly scented herbs, such as coriander, garlic, thyme, and chives. You will also benefit from this because you can pick your herbs up when they are ready and add them to delicious meals.

Another great strategy is crop rotation. This reduces crops' concentration in a particular area and can confuse the pests. It also helps you to manage the fertility of your soil. If you find a specific plant or crop has been overrun with pests, don't plant it in that area or in that raised bed. Instead, move it to another one and place a plant from a different family in its place of it. Interplanting is another excellent way to stave off pests. Most pests will enjoy motocross. This means that all the plants and crops in that area are exactly the same. You can put rows of vegetables next to rows of insect-attracting and pest-repelling flowers and herbs. This way, you get to protect your crops. You can also think about getting floating row covers. A row cover will allow light and water to get through, but it keeps the pests out. You might only need these while your plants are quite young because when they are fully grown, they will be much more resistant.

One important thing to remember is that one or two pests are not the world's end. It is a good thing to have a few pests in your garden. It is completely natural because there are natural enemies to these pests that will be attracted to the area because they can feed. Without a few pests in your garden, beneficial insects will not want to stay. It would help if you always kept an eye on the number of pests you have but never freak out until you genuinely have an infestation or there are signs of it coming.

Once you have an infestation on your hands, it is time to start taking drastic action. The first thing that you want to do is remove the infested plant from the area. This will help keep it from spreading to other healthy plants. Many people are not big fans of treating their plans with pesticides because of the chemicals that can get into them. However, if you want to use pesticides, then it is better to remove the infested plants and use them on them. This way, you do not have to infect the rest of the plants.

It is always better to be proactive rather than reactive when you are already dealing with the problem. When you have a pest outbreak, then think about it as a learning opportunity to help you grow in your gardening abilities. You can always return to the section and go through the specific actions you should be taking. If you have done this, then there will be a lower chance that you have to deal with large outbreaks in the future. It is also a good idea to track the pests you see. When you can see one or two of them, make a note of what they are. If you know what they are, you can start thinking of a plan to get rid of them if it becomes serious. You might want to use biological control made explicitly for that pest, or you might want to introduce natural enemies to that pest in advance. This is all going to be a learning experience, and you will get better with time.

Common Diseases

We have already gone through the various types of pests that you would have to deal with. Now we are going through the common diseases you might see in your garden. One of the most common diseases is called black spots. This is often found on roses, but it can be found on many other plants. You will usually find it on ornamental garden plants rather than crops. As the name suggests, you will find black, round spots on the top of your leaves. The lower leaves will be infected first, and then it moves up. If the infestation gets very serious, the leaves will turn yellow and fall off the plant. This disease is most common during wet periods. If your leaves are wet for more than six hours a day, then you can expect to see this disease creeping in. If you know this disease on your plants, start chopping off the affected leaves. You also must ensure that your plant is as dry as possible in the leafy areas. Making sure that your soil is well-draining and has been fertilized is also an excellent step to take. Water will spread this disease, so make sure that you do not put any water on the leaves. If you are dealing with a lot of rain, it is a good idea to cover your plants when it rains to protect them from this.

You might find that other leaf spots are popping up on your plant. These can be caused by fungal leaf spot disease. This can be found on pretty much any plant, and it generally occurs during the wet and warm seasons or conditions. The same steps should be taken for these kinds of spots as with the black spots. Most spot diseases that you find on your plant are going to be due to fungal infections. Fungi love the wet and warm weather. Make sure you are more aware of this during these seasons.

Mildew is something else that you will have to look out for. This is also a fungal disease, and it looks like a powdery white patch that forms on the leaves. This powdery, white substance can be found anywhere on the plant, even on the stems. This fungus will thrive if you have low soil moisture and high humidity. If your plants are kept in the shade, they will be more suscep-tible to this disease than those in direct sunlight. It is always a good idea to inspect any plants you purchase from a greenhouse or gardening store to ensure that there isn't any powdery mildew on them. The best thing to do is to trim and remove the plants that have this fungus on them. Any debris that has fallen off or that you chop off should be thrown away, and do not use them as a compost. This could spread the disease. You also want to space your plants far enough away so that there is an increase of air circulation and not as much humidity.

Another type of mildew that you should look out for is called downy mildew. This type of mildew is more related to algae and will produce grey, fuzzy-looking spores. This usually appears on the lower surfaces of the leaves. This type of mildew usually occurs when the weather is cool and moist. So this will be early in the springtime or late in the fall. Downy mildew needs water in order to spread and survive. If there's no water on your leaves, then it will not spread. This means that you need to make sure that your leaves are dry. You should also chop off any of the diseased leaves and throw them away.

The next disease we are going to be talking about is called blight. This is also a fungal disease that is spread through windborne spores. This means that the infection can spread incredibly quickly. You will usually find these in warm and humid conditions. There is no cure for these fungal infections, so you must prevent them. Potatoes are particularly prone to these types of fungi. It is best to grow early varieties so that you can harvest them before midsummer when blight tends to be at its worst. If you notice any infected plants, you need to cut off the infected areas immediately. Throw them away and do not compost them.

Canker is a fungal or bacterial pathogen that creates an open wound on the plant. Some of these can be serious, and others not so much. You will usually find these on W=woody landscape plants. Some symptoms are swollen, sunken, cracked, or dead areas found on limbs, trunks, and stems. If your plants have been weakened due to stress from cold, insects, drought, or not getting enough nutrients, then they will be more susceptible to cankers. If you notice that this disease has taken hold of your plants, it is best to remove any diseased plants and areas and destroy them. Try and get resistant varieties whenever possible and avoid overwatering and overcrowding your garden. It is also a good idea to be very careful with your garden so as not to cause any harm. Remember, any stress put onto your plants will make them more susceptible to diseases.

Dealing With Diseases in Your Garden

After you've worked so hard on your garden, it can be incredibly demotivating when you find a disease that has stricken them. However, even the healthiest gardens fall victim to certain conditions, just like how even the healthiest person can fall ill or get a cold or flu. It is just something that we have to deal with as gardeners. The best cure for a disease is always going to be prevention, but sometimes that's not enough. In this case, you should have a plan of action ready.

Nearly all fungicides are to be used as protection and not cure any disease your plants may have. You will have to use them before or as soon as the pathogen strikes. If the disease has already taken hold, it will be very difficult to reverse it. In this case, you will have to take more drastic measures. The best thing to do is to pay close attention to your garden in the very wet months. When you have excessive rain and wet seasons, ensure you are constantly looking at your plants. This will help you to catch anything right at the beginning so that you can take action.

If you have waited too long and the pathogen has taken hold of your plants in a way that has affected the yield or even the aesthetics of your garden, you might have to step in with some products to control the disease. You have to choose these products wisely and do your research on them. You need to know whether the disease is bacterial or fungal. There will be different products for each. If you use a fungicide on a bacterial disease, you're not going to see any results. This could leave you feeling very frustrated, and the disease will get progressively worse. You must first identify the disease before stepping in with products to help you. If you're having problems identifying the disease, cut off one of the leaves that have been affected and take it to a local gardening shop or plant nursery. They will be able to help you identify what it is, and you can get a plan from there.

If you use synthetic or chemical-based products, you have to do so with care. These things can be damaging and should only be used as a last resort. You need to follow the instructions on the package exactly as it is printed, and you'll also need to protect yourself accordingly.

There are also a few natural fungicides that you could use in your garden if you are not looking to use some-thing synthetic or chemical-based. Bicarbonates are an excellent choice, and these include things like potas-sium bicarbonate, sodium bicarbonate, and ammonium bicarbonate. The potassium and ammonium bicarbonate-based products show better results than regular baking soda or sodium bicarbonate. Bicarbonates will work when you place them directly on the fungus by inhibiting its growth by damaging its cell walls. There is a very low toxicity rate with these types of products. It is basically nonexistent, so it is usually very safe. You can find bicarbonate-based disease control at your local plant store.

Bacillus subtilis is a biological fungicide that can also be used. This can be found naturally occurring in soil and even in the gut of a human. This is a living organism, so you are using one living organism to manage another. This bacteria will inhibit the support germination of the fungus. You can also use this against specific bacterial pathogens. The great thing about using this is that there are no negative impacts on other living species. You can find products with this in them at your local gardening store.

Other products that you could try are copper-based products. These usually come in sprays. You have to be careful with this because some plants have adverse reactions to it. When copper ions reach the surface of a plant, they destroy the pathogens before they can even enter the plant's tissue. However, once the disease has become symptomatic (you can see the spots or the marks on the leaves and stems), you can no longer use this spray. You need to use this as a type of preventative measure. If you know that your garden is susceptible to diseases, you can use the spray for prevention and protection. Most copper-based products are certified as organic and can be used in organic agriculture, but if they are ingested or inhaled, they can be highly toxic. If the copper builds up in your soil, then this could also negatively impact the earth's worms. This can be bad for your soil's health, so you have to be careful when using this.

Sulfur-based products are another popular option. This is another preventative fungicide because it prevents the spores from first taking hold of your plant. You should not use sulfur-based products when the temperature is consistently above 80°F. You can ask your local garden shop for some advice and help to find sulfur-based products. Neem oil is something else that can be used. This can be used as a pesticide and a fungicide. Again, this is more preventative than used to solve a problem that has already taken root. Two other options are products containing Streptomyces griseoviridis and Streptomyces lydicus, and Trichoderma harzianum.

When trying to handle diseases in your garden, you need to make sure that you do everything in your power to prevent them from taking hold in the first place. This means you must ensure that your garden doesn't continuously stay wet because diseases love warm and damp environments. Allowing airflow to go through your garden is also really important. This means you need to space out each of your plants appropriately, so they are not clumped together. This will also help slow down the spread of the diseases. If plants are spread out, they can't jump from plant to plant as quickly. It is also vital that you analyze your plants now and then to know what's going on with them. If you can pick up on the disease as soon as possible, it will be much easier for you to handle.

5

PLANNING WHAT TO PLANT

K nowing what kind of fruit, vegetables, and plants you want to place in your garden can be challenging. There are so many choices out there, and it is really important that you make the right ones. Some plants will take more effort from you, so you need to know what you can handle. There are also some plants that are more resistant to diseases and pests, and these kinds of plants are a little bit lower in maintenance. You'll have to take into account your climate and what grows well in the weather conditions. There is a lot to consider, but we will go through all of this in this chapter.

WHEN TO BEGIN PLANTING

One of the biggest questions that people have is when they should begin planting. It would help if you did this at the right time of year to get fruits and vegetables at their peak tenderness. In most cases, you will begin sowing your seeds in spring so they can fully mature by summer. With this being said, there are certain vegetables that need to be sown a little earlier. Some plants are best started from inside and then moved outdoors. This means that you will take care of your plants indoors until they have sprouted, and then you can move them outside. Most of these transplanted seeds will grow faster and produce fruit and vegetables much quicker than those just placed in the soil outside. In general, summer crops and those with a longer growing season should be sown indoors, while crops that will mature in the fall can be directly sown outside.

You must be prepared to start your seeds just as spring rolls around. In general, you need to start sowing your seeds about 4 to 6 weeks before the last frost date. It is helpful to look at the seed packet as this will give you a good indication of when you need to start. Most seed packets will also give you detailed instructions on how to do it and what is the best method. The best time to start your seeds is from late March until late May. If you live in warmer southern climates, you can begin planting a bit earlier. Since there is some variation based on where you live, it is important to get some advice from professionals. You are also likely to find this advice on the seed packets. Many of them are targeted to your area so that you can get the best results from your seeds.

A few seeds that should be started earlier are:

- Broccoli
- Cabbage
- Lettuce
- Cauliflower

These should be sown about ten weeks before the date of the last frost. They take a lot longer and should be planted inside before moving them outdoors. Tomatoes, eggplant, and peppers are more warm-season plants, which means you can plant them seven weeks before the last frost. Melons and cucurbits can be planted for weeks before the last frost.

INTERPLANTING

Let's talk about interplanting. You may or may not have heard of this term before, but it is an important thing to know about if you want to grow a healthy garden. Not everybody has to do it, but it is a valuable tool to have in your arsenal when you are starting a garden. This is a pretty old method that has proven successful throughout the years. It will allow you to grow many different crops in a small garden. It also enhances the fertility of the soil and can improve the plant's health by promoting cooperation through different species.

This might sound all well and good, but I'm sure you're still wondering what interplanting actually is. In the most basic terms, interplanting is just choosing a few different plants to plant in the same space. For example, you must pair tall plants with shorter ones that can go under them. Basically, you are pairing up different kinds of plants so that you can repel pests and reap many other benefits. You are not going to have a single raised garden bed with only one type of plant. You're going to choose a few plants to grow in one area so that you can get the maximum benefit from it. You will also find that doing this reduces diseases and pests. For example, you can plant nitrogen-rich plants such as beans, along with other types of plants, such as other vegetables, various fruits, herbs, and flowers. The nitrogen that is being imparted into the soil will help your other plants grow bigger and stronger.

You first have to think about what plants you want to grow. It would help if you also did your research on the various plants to see which ones will work best together. You also need to understand what kind of challenges you are going to face with your garden because you want to make sure that the plants you do integrate are going to flourish. You can consider pairing up two very different plants. For example, certain plants like carrots, tomatoes, and parsnips are deeply rooted. On the other hand, you have shallow vegetables such as lettuce, potatoes, and broccoli. These two things can be planted together because they're not going to compete for root space. You can also choose to plant something like corn which is a slow-maturing plant, along with something that grows a lot faster, such as spinach. If you are growing tall plants, then you can take advantage of the bottom space by planting things like celery, spinach, and lettuce.

COMPANION PLANTING

Companion planting is pretty similar to interplanting. You are going to be planting certain plants that are going to be providing benefits to one another. This means that each plant will complement another, and they will receive an extended amount of benefits. This helps them to grow by attracting good insects and repelling the bad ones. You could also do this in a way that sacrifices one of the plants so that it can lure a hungry pest away from the ones that you want to grow.

There are many ways you can use companion planting to your advantage. The first one is based on reduced competition. For example, you can plant a vegetable with deep roots next to one with shallow roots. They will not be competing for nutrients since the roots are at different levels of the soil. Another way is to improve the soil. Some plants will improve the soil quality of other plants. For example, nitrogen-rich plants such as beans can be planted alongside other fruits and vegetables to increase the soil quality. The next one is used as a pest repellent. We have already spoken about multiple different herbs and plants that repel certain pests. If you plant these alongside other fruits and vegetables, you can stave off unwanted guests from your fruit and vegetables.

SUCCESSION PLANTING

Succession planting is a standard method that allows you to continuously have maturing fruits and vegetables. You can extend your harvest by staggering your planting or by planting a variety of fruits and vegetables that will mature at different times. There are a variety of ways in which you can implement succession planting in your garden.

The first way is to use the same vegetable or fruit but stagger the planting. You will space out the plantings of the same vegetable over the course of a few weeks. For example, you might be planting onions, and every 2 to 4 weeks, you will plant new ones. Instead of planting all your onions at the same time, you will plant them in smaller amounts and at different times. Many vegetables fade after producing their first crop. You'll get a heavy yield at first and then smaller and smaller yields as the time go on. This means that you will have plenty of crops all at one time and then no crops afterwards. This is usually not ideal for somebody who has a home garden. If you plant in succession, then you can harvest every few weeks. A new crop will continuously be coming in.

The next way you can implement succession planting is by using different vegetables with short growing seasons. Peas, carrots, beets, basil, arugula, dill, green onions, kale, and spinach have very short growing seasons. This means that you could plant one thing at the beginning of the growing season, harvest it, and then plant something different. You will still get to repeat these vegetables even though they are ready at different times. It'll give you some variety in your vegetables.

The final way to keep your harvest from coming in continuously over the growing season is to plant different vegetables that mature at different rates. Some vegetables will mature much earlier, and others will mature much later. If you want to reap continuously, you should look at different vegetables that mature at various stages of spring and summer. You can find out this information by looking at the seed packets. Often they will say how long you can expect to be waiting before your seeds mature into fully grown vegetables.

CROP ROTATION

Crop rotation is a very popular growing technique, and all it means is that you will be planting different crops sequentially in your garden to improve the health of your soil and optimize the amount of nutrients it has. Crop rotation also aids in pest and weed repelling. For example, you might start by planting corn, and once the corn has reached maturity and you harvest it, then you will replace all your corn plants with beans or legumes. The legumes will add nitrogen to the soil to be ready for the next crop. You also have the benefit of being able to harvest the beans.

You will probably be able to rotate two or three different crops in a season. Doing this will also help you to keep away the pests and weeds. Pests often enjoy staying with gardens that only grow the same thing. This is because certain pests enjoy certain types of fruit or vegetables. If you have a pest that has an affinity for tomatoes and all you grow are tomatoes, then you're probably going to have an issue with these pests. However, if you grow tomatoes and then, once they have matured, choose to grow something else, these pests will not have enough time to gain a foothold in your garden. Crop rotation is an excellent way to get a wide variety of fruit and vegetables in a small garden as well as keep the soil and garden area healthy.

SEEDS VS SEEDLINGS

When you are creating a garden, you are going to have the choice of either choosing to start from scratch with seeds or to plant seedlings. There are pros and cons to both of these, and it is important to understand what they are so you can make an informed decision. The main difference between the two is that with seeds, which you can buy from the store or get from a fruit or vegetable to plant directly into your garden, and you will have complete control from the beginning.

On the other hand, a seedling is something that you can buy from a plant nursery. This seedling will be an already sprouted seed, and it is basically just a small version of the plant you want to grow. If you choose to start with a seed, you need to be prepared for the length of time it will take to grow. Seeds do take a much longer time to mature into full-grown plants. Since seedlings have already sprouted, if you purchase these, then you'll have skipped the entire first step of growing a plant. This means that you can get your matured plants sooner. If you are worried about starting at the seed phase, then you might want to consider purchasing a few seedlings. Since a lot of the legwork is done for you, you do not have to worry so much. Seedlings can also be a good option if you have started later on in the growing period. When you are using seeds to grow your plants, you will have to start planting before the winter ends. However, this is not the case when you use seedlings. You won't be able to start your garden a bit later since you are skipping the seed step.

Something else that you should consider is the price. Often, seeds are much cheaper than seedlings. You can get seeds for a very small amount of money, and in many cases, you can get them for free. If you have fruits and vegetables in your house, then you have seeds. You can use these seeds to start planting, and it will not cost you anything more. Seedlings will cost you a bit more money since somebody else has done the work to nurture the seeds and allow them to sprout. Most of the time, the seedlings will not cost you an arm and a leg, but it really depends on what kind of plant you want to grow and where you buy them from.

DOUBLE DIGGING

As we now know, healthy soil is key to a healthy garden. Many different aspects come into play when trying to increase your soil's health. In most cases, when you can't find healthy soil, you have to make it. This is where double digging comes into play. If you still want to use the soil already in your yard or on your property, then this might be a really good way to increase the soil quality so that you can transplant it into your raised bed garden.

When you double dig, you are removing the top layer of the soil so that you expose the subsoil or the hard part of the soil that is beneath it. Then you take your shovel and break it up and then add organic matter. Once that is done, you will replace the topsoil you have already removed. This automatically increases the quality of your soil and makes it so the roots can dig in much deeper. You can leave it like this for a short time and then transplant the soil into your garden.

This a very simple technique that can help you improve the quality of your soil by a significant amount. If you choose to make a raised bed garden that still has access to the soil on the ground, this could be an excellent technique to use, even if you're not going to transplant the soil into the raised bed garden itself. The roots of your plants will be able to dig even deeper into the ground so they can be strong and healthy. You'll find that your plants are a lot healthier just because your soil has a lot more nutrients in it.

6

HOW TO PLANT FRUITS AND VEGETABLES

F ruits and vegetables are the most popular plants to grow in a raised bed garden. This is because they provide you with food, and it is incredibly rewarding to grow your own. Once you have started growing vegetables in your garden, you will not want to turn back. You will also find that the food you grow yourself tastes so much better just based on the principle that you did the hard work yourself. Not only that, but you can be sure that it is organic and has not been grown in a way that leaves any nasty pesticides or chemicals in it.

GROWING VEGETABLES IN RAISED GARDEN BEDS

Some vegetables grow better in a raised bed garden than others. You can try and grow as many different types of vegetables as you would like, but as raised bed gardening has become popular, people can suss out which are the best for raised bed gardening. There are so many vegetables to choose from, and this can make it really exciting to grow them. Each vegetable is different, so it does pay to do specific research on the types you are interested in growing. With that being said, here's a list of some of the best vegetables to grow in a raised bed garden:

Radishes: These are great vegetables for beginners because they grow quickly. If fast results are what you're looking for, then you really can't go wrong with a radish. You would probably be able to see them appearing at about the four-week mark after sowing. This means you can quickly get a constant supply throughout the spring and summer months. Make sure you are not growing them too close together; otherwise, you'll get small radishes.

Chard: This is quite an easy-to-grow vegetable for a raised bed garden. The best environment for this is a sunny one that has nourishing soil. You can plant the seeds, and once they start growing, you will cut the leaves off. You do not need to re-plant the sources each time because you are just using the leaves. Every time you cut them, more will grow, and you'll have a constant supply with little effort.

Onions: Some people are incredibly huge fans of the onion, but others don't really have a taste for it. If you fall on the former side, you would be pleased to know that onions are quite easy to grow in a raised bed garden. An onion's roots can be long, so make sure there is quite a bit of space underneath once you plant the seed. You really only need to make a small hole in the soil with your finger and place the seed in. Cover up that hole, and you will be set to have delicious onions in the next few weeks.

Spinach: Almost everyone enjoys eating spinach in one way or another. It is an incredibly easy vegetable to include in your meals and your general diet. You will be able to reap spinach leaves throughout the whole year, except when it starts to frost.

Tomatoes: These are undoubtedly one of the most common vegetables that people enjoy growing. This is because they are very versatile, and you can use them in almost every meal. You do not need your soil to be extremely deep as long as you have enough space for the roots to spread out. The roots of the tomato plant can grow horizontally. This means that even if you have a very shallow raised bed garden, you can definitely grow tomatoes.

Garlic: If you are somebody who adds garlic to everything, then you will be pleased to know that this is an excellent addition to a raised bed garden. All you need to do is use the individual cloves of garlic as your seeds. You plant each clove individually with the pointy end up. You need to ensure that there is a period of cold for them to start growing. This means the best time to plant is in November or December. By the time spring rolls around, you will be able to start harvesting your new garlic bulbs.

Cucumbers: Almost everybody eats cucumbers so that they can make a perfect addition to your raised bed garden. The two varieties are the bush and vine varieties. You can grow either one of them depending on how much space you have in your garden or whatever your preferences are.

This is by no means an exhaustive list of vegetables you can grow in your garden. There are many more, but these are the most popular and some of the easiest to grow in a raised bed garden set-up. You could also try to grow vegetables that are a bit more difficult. It is going to take you some time to get it right, but you can basically grow anything in a raised bed garden that you could grow in a regular one.

GROWING FRUIT IN RAISED GARDEN BEDS

There are many fruits that you can plant in your raised bed garden. However, you should always choose the fruit that you enjoy eating. There is no point in growing a bunch of fruits in your garden and not wanting to enjoy them. At the end of the day, your raised bed garden is going to be about what you want to eat.

One thing you have to be aware of is that the homegrown fruit will not look as picture-perfect as the ones you buy at the store. Most of the fruits that come from the store have been picked specifically to look their best so that people will buy them. On top of that, a lot of them are genetically modified to make them look brighter, bigger, or shaped more appealingly. Don't be surprised when some of your fruit is smaller, oddly colored, and just doesn't look the same as the store-bought fruit. There is nothing wrong with your fruit, this is actually how they are naturally supposed to look. Here is a list of some of the best fruit plants to grow in your raised bed garden:

Apple trees: Apples are one of the best fruits to grow for beginner gardeners. There are plenty of varieties of apples, so make sure that you grow the apples that you enjoy eating. Apple trees do need cross-pollination to fertilize. This means that you should plant at least one or two different partner trees close by. You will also need to ensure that you are pruning your apple trees at the right time so that your trees produce lots of fruit. Once your apple tree has been established and is growing, then it's going to be very low maintenance. You'll just have to prune yearly, add fertilizer to the base, and you will be able to enjoy the fruit in 2 to 3 years.

Fig tree: Eating homegrown figs can feel like a luxury or like you are royalty. They are absolutely delicious, and the good news is that they grow amazingly in a raised bed garden. You can add them to any meal, including salads, desserts, sauces, or baked goods. You will need to ensure that your fig tree has access to plenty of sunlight so the fruit can ripen. If you grow it against a wall, this restricts root growth; this might not sound like a good thing, but when this happens, the fruit starts to increase its yield. Since they do not need a large space to grow, fig-trees will make an excellent raised bed garden fruit.

Lemon trees: Not only are the fruit of lemons amazing and versatile, but the smell of the trees in the spring and summertime is absolutely to die for. It makes your garden feel fresh and lively. Growing them in a pot is a great way to help your lemon tree thrive in colder climates. Lemon trees prefer warmer weather, so you do need to be conscious of this and make sure that you're not allowing too much of the cold to get in. Investing in a citrus feed for your lemon trees is a good idea since they need a lot of nutrients to thrive success-fully. Pruning your lemon tree will result in a higher fruit yield, so make sure that you are cutting off dead leaves, bad fruit, or decaying branches.

Plum trees: Plum trees are a great option because they produce a lot of fruit. You can also make jams and spreads with these fruits, as well as just enjoy them whole. These trees are quite small, so you don't have to worry about them taking up a lot of space. You could consider purchasing one that is a dwarf rootstock. This means that it is grafted from a smaller tree root so that the size of the plant is controlled. You will still get a good amount of fruit from this type of tree, all that has been controlled is the height and the width of the actual tree. You will need to get a partner tree for cross-pollination. With this being said, some varieties can be grown on their own. These include the Victoria and Majorie's seedling varieties. Make sure you have a chat with your plant nursery staff so that they can give you the best advice regarding this. When growing a plum tree, you need to ensure that the location is warm and sheltered, and the soil needs to retain a good amount of moisture.

Mulberry tree: Mulberries are incredibly delicious berries, but they are very rarely sold in stores. If you do want to enjoy them, then it is best to grow this fruit for yourself. If you have never tried a mulberry, then it can be compared to the flavor of a blackberry, but there is still a distinct flavor that comes with it. The actual tree is very beautiful and makes a great addition to your garden. You can get many varieties of tree that grows either red, black, or white berries. With this being said, only the red and black berries are grown to enjoy for food. The actual tree is quite fast-growing, but it takes a while to produce fruit. If you grow your mulberry tree in a pot or a raised bed garden, this can reduce the time you have to wait for the fruit to grow. They are quite tolerant plants, so you don't have to be as strict with the soil type that you grow them in; they can even handle partly shady conditions. One thing you must be conscious of is that these berries can stain the ground below them. It is wise to not plant a mulberry tree close to walkways or paving, otherwise, you'll end up having a lot of red and black stains on the ground. It would help if you also were cautious of not letting birds feed on the crop. This can stain the bird's feces which will, in turn, leave stains wherever they defecate.

Cherry trees: A cherry tree has to be one of the most enchanting trees in the entire world. Not only are the fruits delicious, but the beautiful blossoms in the springtime are stunning. You will get these light pink blossoms in the springtime, followed by bright red berries in the summer. You will also have an amazing color from these trees in fall. These trees are incredibly low maintenance and one of the easiest-to-grow fruit trees you can have in your garden. You can also grow a dwarf rootstock, so you don't have to deal with a massive tree in your garden. This means that it is perfect for raised bed gardens or smaller pots. You will need to ensure that the soil is fertile and that you water it regularly until the tree has been fully established. Once the tree has fully grown, then it will be low main-tenance. If you want to grow sweet varieties, you will be growing them in a sunny area, but if you have decided on more sour varieties, you'll need to plant them in a shady location. Pruning is also vital when it comes to a cherry tree. This will ensure that you have a high yield of fruit when the growing season arrives.

Peachtree: If you are looking for a low-maintenance fruit tree, then the peach tree is right up your alley. You could also grow nectarines, just the smooth variety of peaches. They grow the same way, so there's not too much variety in how you need to take care of them. A peach tree produces fruit quickly, so you might find that your tree gives you some delicious peaches within a year of planting. Most other trees take quite a long time before they start producing fruit. When it comes to soil, your peach tree isn't going to be as fancy as many other types of trees. Just make sure that it has good drainage and that you have positioned it in a place with a lot of sunlight. If you live in an area prone to frost, you don't have to worry too much because peaches tend to flower early in the season. This means they are not going to be too affected by colder weather.

When it comes to fruit, it is best to grow what you are going to enjoy eating. This means that your garden will yield something that is actually rewarding. Don't only look at what's going to produce the most fruit or what's going to be the easiest to grow, because at the end of the day, if you do not like that fruit, then there is no point in going forward with it. You also need to be sure of whether your fruit trees are self-pollinating or not. If they are not self-pollinating, you will need to plant at least two of the same or same variety of trees for your fruit to grow.

GROWING HERBS

Herbs make a great addition to your garden because they can literally be added to any meal. You can say goodbye to bland cooking when you have a variety of herbs at your disposal. The other great thing about herbs is that they are so easy to grow, and there are so many varieties out there. You will definitely be able to find quite a few that fit your cooking style and tastes.

Different herbs will require different growing environments. This means that you can't just randomly group herbs together in the same garden. You will need to cater to your herbs' needs to get the best results from them. Some herbs are drought tolerant and ones that love water. You'll see better results if you group herbs from either of these categories in separate pots or raised bed gardens. Some drought-tolerant herbs are thyme, rosemary, lavender, sage, oregano, and chamomile. Some water-loving herbs are parsley, cilantro, basil, mint, saffron, chives, and cumin. We will go through a few tips and tricks you can use to grow a successful and thriving herb garden.

Pick the Right Location

Choosing the right location to plant your garden is incredibly important. Most herbs love to be in full sunlight for as long as possible. This is why it's incredibly important to choose a location with at least 6 to 8 hours of sunlight per day. In the summertime, when the sun is in full force, it can be a good idea to provide shade in the afternoon heat. The morning and evening sun is perfectly fine for herbs.

Be sure to also read the instructions on the seed packet to see the needs of each specific herb. This will allow you to provide the best environment for the types of herbs that you have purchased and are looking to grow. Herbs are pretty resilient, so they are not as tricky as many other plants, and this means that you don't have to be overly worried about them.

Herbs tend to spread like wildfire, so if you do not contain them properly, they will keep growing as wide as possible. You are already containing them in some way when you build a raised bed garden, but if you are looking to have many different herbs in one bed, then you need to make a plan. You will have to separate each herb by lining your raised bed with something like patio stones or something similar. Each herb will have its own section of the raised bed and will not be able to spread.

Drainage is Important

Using soil with a good amount of drainage will be incredibly important. When soil is very dense and does not allow water to permeate through it, it will enable fungal diseases to take root in your herbs. It can be challenging to deal with fungal diseases once they have hold of your herbs, and this is why it is better to make sure that you're doing what you can to prevent them.

It is a good idea to check the moisture level of your soil before watering it again. If you place your finger about an inch or two deep into the soil and feel that it is still wet, then there is no need for you to water it. Many people make the mistake of looking at the top layer of soil to determine whether they should water the herbs or not. The problem with this is that the top layer will usually always be dried out quite quickly. This is especially so when you have plants that are in direct sunlight. With herbs, sunlight is incredibly important, so the chances of the top layer of soil drying out quite quickly is high. Checking the moisture level in the inner layers of soil will be a much better tell so that you know whether you should water or not.

Don't be in a Rush to Plant

If you want to grow herbs, you need to be patient. Many people want to jumpstart the growing season and plant as soon as they see springtime rolling around. While this may sound like a fantastic idea, the truth is that herbs do not like the cold and do not like frost. Frost and cold temperatures can decimate your herb garden. This is why you must wait until the weather starts to warm up properly. You want the night temperatures to remain over 50°F before you can think about planting your herbs.

Herbs grow quickly, so you don't have to stress that you're not going to have herbs in the growing season. You could also choose to buy herbs that are already grown and just transplant them into your garden. You don't even have to go to a plant nursery for this. Your regular grocery store will have some herbs that have just been pulled out of the ground. You can simply plant some of these and watch them grow.

GROWING FLOWERS

Everybody loves to see a garden blooming and blossoming with flowers. Not only are they beautiful to look at, but they bring about a fresh and sweet smell to your garden. You might not know which flowers are best for the raised bed garden, but this is precisely what this section will be about. We are going to go through a few of the best flowers that you can grow in a raised bed garden so that they will flourish:

Sedum: This is a beautiful flower you can add to your garden. It is star-shaped, which makes it really unique.

You'll be able to sprout these flowers from the beginning of spring all the way until autumn. If you love butterflies, this is a great way to attract them to your garden. It will bring life and vibrancy to any raised bed.

Agastache: If you live in an arid climate, then this is a great choice of flower for you. Other names for it are hummingbird mint or hyssop. I'm sure you've heard something similar before. These are very drought-tolerant plants, and you'll be able to get flowers in many different colors.

Erigeron karvinskianus: The colloquial name for this plant is the Mexican daisy. It is a wonderful flowering plant that will add a softness to your flower bed. It has white and pink blossoms. Another positive that comes around with this type of flower is that it is drought tolerant and can withstand drier temperatures.

French lavender: Almost everybody appreciates the smell of lavender because it's calming and soothing. Not only that, but its purple color is extremely beautiful to look at, and it stands out from the rest of the flowers. If you're looking to inject a different color and shape into your flower garden, this is a great flower to do it with. French lavender does not need much care or water, so you can grow very healthy plants without putting in a lot of effort.

Penstemon: This flower is also called the beardtongue. Despite the strange name, this is a beautiful flower that comes in various colors. This means that it is very popular with many gardeners. One thing to note is that this plant has a shorter lifespan than many other flowers we have already mentioned. However, this has not taken away from its popularity. It is definitely worth it to try out this flower and see how it looks in your garden once it blossoms.

Planting fruit, vegetables, herbs, and flowers are the best part of creating a raised bed garden. You'll be able to reap the rewards because you can see the tangible results, whether this be delicious fruits and vegetables, fragrant herbs, or beautiful flowers. Once you get into raised bed gardening, you might want to start playing around with different plants. While you might have started thinking about only growing flowers, you could expand your gardening knowledge into other things like herbs or vegetables. They require slightly different skills, but you can also find some low-maintenance plants. Remember to start small and then continue growing a garden according to how much space, time, and resources you have.

7

COMMON MISTAKES

There are some common mistakes that people make when they are planning and building their raised bed garden. These mistakes are pretty easy to fix or prevent, and it is far better to prevent mistakes than to do it and have to work on rectifying the situation. As you are planning and constructing your raised bed, think about whether you are making these mistakes. Knowing what they are will make you more aware as you create your raised bed garden.

PICKING THE WRONG SPOT

One of the most important decisions you will make when you start your raised bed garden is picking the spot. Your garden should receive enough sunlight so that your plants can grow and be healthy. This means it should receive at least six hours of direct sunlight daily. It is a good idea to pick a relatively flat area. If you select a low-lying area, there is a higher chance that the hills will create shadows over your garden, and rainwater can collect here. You should also avoid putting your raised bed up against a wall because you won't have access from all four sides. This can be a hindrance when trying to maintain and take care of your garden.

The best thing to do is look at your outdoor space. See where the sun falls and what shade is being cast over your outdoor space throughout the day. Consider that you will have different shadows cast into your garden in different seasons. For example, in winter, most trees and bushes will be stripped of their leaves. This means that there is not going to be a lot of shade in certain areas of your yard. On the other hand, in the summer, when your plants and trees are in full bloom, there will be a lot more shade in some regions of your yard.

FORGETTING ABOUT A WATER SOURCE

There is not much we can do regarding where a water source is placed. Chances are, you already have an outside tap that has been installed. You have to consider where your water source is and then plan your raised bed garden around this. It would be incredibly frustrating to have to fill up large buckets of water and lug them across the property in order to water your raised bed garden. If you choose to use an irrigation system, placing your raised bed far away from the tap will mean you have to purchase a lot more tubing. Not only does this cost more money, but it can be an eyesore to have large amounts of tubing running throughout your yard.

Take a moment to consider where your water source is, and then plan around that.

MAKING THE BEDS TOO BIG

One of the biggest mistakes that you can make when building a raised bed is making it too big. Many people become incredibly excited about the prospect of building a raised bed garden and become too optimistic about the size they can handle. Having a raised bed that is too big will hinder you from taking care of the plants when they are growing. You should never have a raised bed garden that you can't reach halfway across from one side. You need to be able to tend to the plants that are in the middle. About 3 to 5 feet wide is the ideal width of a raised bed. Of course, if you are taller or shorter than average, you do have to take this into consideration, but that width does work for most people.

You also have to take into consideration how long the raised bed is. You do not want to walk in large circles to care for your garden. It is far better to have a few smaller raised beds than one really big one. Remember, you cannot step into your raised bed garden, so if you make it too big, there will be patches that you will not be able to reach and take care of. If you choose a premade kit for your raised bed garden, it will be an appropriate size for most people to handle.

BUILDING WITH THE WRONG MATERIALS

One of the most important decisions you will make when building your raised bed garden is the type of materials that you will be using. You want to use materials that will stand the test of time and will not cost you down the road. You also have to be sure that whatever materials you are using will not leach toxic chemicals and materials into your soil. This can have serious repercussions, not only for the plants but for you if you eat the fruit and vegetables from them.

We have already gone through the types of materials that you should be using and the ones you should be avoiding. If you need a little refresher feel free to go back to Chapter 3 and review the relevant sections again. This will help you understand what materials you should purchase and which ones you should stay away from. There is no point in buying cheap material and having to replace the whole thing the following year.

SELECTING THE WRONG SOIL

The health of the soil you choose to use will have a massive impact on the health of the plants you grow in your raised bed garden. One of the biggest misconceptions is that you can just pick up any bag of garden soil and dump it into your raised bed. Most bags of garden soil are designed to be mixed into existing soil already on your ground. Since you are building a raised bed, there will not be any of this existing topsoil. If you were just to dump a whole bag of garden soil into your raised bed, there is a big chance that it can become compacted, and this will inhibit drainage. This means that water will stand and not seep through, and this can be dangerous for your plants.

When you go into the gardening store to buy soil, make sure it has been designed for raised beds. The soil would be mixed with regular topsoil so that it is not as dense as regular fertilized garden soil. This will be much healthier for your plants. If you are unsure what you should use, then feel free to speak to the employees at your local garden store. They will be able to guide you in the right direction, and you can ask them any questions that you might have regarding your raised bed garden. In most cases, you will be able to find a very friendly staff member who can offer you some specific advice for your climate and gardening goals.

SELECTING OVERSIZED PLANTS

When you have a raised bed garden, you have limited space to plant and grow your fruits and vegetables. If you choose massive plants, you will quickly run out of space, which can cause overcrowding in your garden bed. Before you decide which plants you want to add to your raised garden, you need to do some research to see their full size. Certain plants, like zucchini plants, will require an entire raised bed garden for themselves. This means that if you were planning to have only one raised bed garden and want a variety of fruits and vegetables, then a zucchini plant will not be a good choice for you.

It is also essential to understand the space that you're working with. If you have a small yard or outdoor environment, you will not be able to plant large plants. You will also not be able to have multiple individual raised bed gardens. In this case, you need to plant smaller vegetables, herbs, and other plants in your garden. This will allow you to have a lot of variety even though you do not have a lot of space.

SKIPPING MULCH

There is a misconception that you do not need to add mulch to your raised bed garden because it is off the ground. This misconception comes from the fact that people think weeds do not grow in raised gardens. However, this is not true. Even though your garden is not touching the ground, it can still get weeds. Any place where there is plant growth is susceptible to weed growth. Simply adding a layer of mulch will keep the weeds away so that the rest of your plants can thrive.

There are other benefits to mulch as well. Adding a layer of mulch to your soil helps retain the moisture around the roots of your existing plants. This means you don't have to water as often since the ground will be moist. Mulch also keeps your soil dense, which will prevent any rain from splashing soil onto your plants. This will mean that your plants will be a lot cleaner when it is time to pick them and enjoy the fruits of your labor.

NOT PROTECTING YOUR PLANTS

The good news is that you have lifted your garden out of reach from stray rabbits that want to crunch on your delicious produce. The bad news is that there are many other things that your plants need protection from. If you live in an area with a lot of hungry deer, you need to protect your plants from these guys. You might have to install some fencing to repel bigger animals. Stray cats might want to walk through your garden, so spraying some repellent onto the soil can be a good idea. There are also many natural animal repellents that you could use. For some reason, cats don't like the smell of citrus, so you can use this to your advantage by placing orange or lemon peels around the areas you want the cats to stay away from. If you choose to use a chemical repellent or to make something at home, just make sure that it will not be toxic to plants.

NOT PICKING GOOD SOIL

One of the most common mistakes people make is that they just take the native soil from the yard and put it into their raised beds. This might seem like a fantastic idea because the soil is already there, so it's going to be free, but the truth is that this soil might not be the best for plant growth. If you want to use the native soil in your yard, then take the time to test it and ensure that it will be conducive to healthy plant growth. Your soil might be fairly healthy, and all you need to do is amend it to make it work for you. In other cases, you'll find that your soil will not work, and you have to start from scratch.

It is far better to take the time to get suitable soil from the beginning instead of becoming frustrated in the growing season when your plants are not thriving. Soil is the base of a healthy garden, and you need to ensure that this is right. Unless you test your soil or purchase some raised bed garden soil, you'll never know whether your soil is good enough to plant. The only time you will discover this is when spring and summer roll around and your plants are not looking healthy. That would mean you wasted a whole year on something that you could have solved much earlier.

NOT PLANNING YOUR PATHWAYS

If you plan to have more than one raised bed garden, then you need to make sure that you have planned the pathways around each of them. You will need space to walk in the middle of your gardens and kneel so that you can tend to your plants. You will probably also need space for the equipment you will be using. You will probably be wheelbarrowing around some compost or other materials, and it will be incredibly frustrating if you cannot get the wheelbarrow in between your raised bed gardens. What about if you want to mow the lawn and the grass in between your raised bed gardens? You will need enough space for the lawnmower to fit between your raised beds. These are all things that you have to consider before you build your beds.

Take some time and pretend like you're attending to your raised beds. See how much space you need to kneel down and take care of each bed. See if your tools and equipment can fit between each of them. It might seem silly to do now, but it will cause you a lot less stress in the future. It will make everything more accessible when you tend to your garden, and you don't have to carry one small piece of equipment at a time because the space is too small.

NOT AMENDING YOUR SOIL THROUGH THE SEASONS

If you want healthy plants, you will have to take care of the soil as well. It is all well and good to choose the right kind of soil and do your research at the beginning but taking care of soil is an all-year-round thing. You still have to tend to the soil even when you're not actively growing anything. You must remember that soil is living, and if you don't feed it, it will die. This means you will have to start from scratch all over again. It would be best if you planned to add nutrients to the soil between each crop rotation. You should also do this at the end of each growing season. This will make it much easier to maintain healthy soil in your garden. You will find that you'll get into a routine, so it's not going to be too much of a hassle as you get used to it.

8

TRIED AND TESTED RECIPES

Now that you have taken the time to plant and grow some delicious fruits and vegetables, it is time to start enjoying them. The best part of having your garden is the ability to enjoy the food that you grow. There is something special about eating food you have worked hard to produce. It makes every dish you cook taste so much better, and you know that the food will be fresh.

✿ Tomato Fritters

A tomato fritter is a great side dish or a snack. These are crunchy and delicious. You can also make a delicious sauce to go along with them and dip them. Cream cheese or sour cream make delicious dips, so give those a try. These don't keep well for too long, they tend to get soggy. It is best to enjoy them immediately or to pop them into the air fryer or oven to reheat to retain the crispiness.

Time: 30 minutes

Servings: 24

Prep Time: 15 minutes

Cook Time: 15 minutes

Ingredients:

- 1 cup of all-purpose flour
- 1 teaspoon of baking powder
- ½ teaspoon of salt
- Pinch of dried basil

- Pinch dried oregano
- Pinch pepper
- 1 large tomato, chopped
- ½ cup of chopped onion
- ½ cup of Parmesan cheese, grated
- 1 jalapeño pepper, finely chopped (remove seeds if you do not like it spicy)
- 1 garlic clove, minced
- 3 to 5 tablespoons water, optional
- Oil for frying

Directions:

1. Sift the flour, baking powder, and salt into a bowl and then add the pepper, basil, and oregano. Mix it all together.
2. Gently stir the cheese, tomato, onion, jalapeño, and garlic.
3. If the batter seems too thick, you can add 1 tablespoon of water at a time. This will all depend on how much juice comes out of your tomato.
4. Place a nonstick pan or skillet onto the heat. Pour in oil and heat it up to at least 375°F.
5. Dollop tablespoonfuls of batter into the oil. Do not overcrowd the pan, you will need to do this in batches.

6. Fry until the fritters are golden brown. This should take about a minute or two on each side.
7. Remove and place on paper towels to drain the excess oil.
8. Enjoy warm.

✿ Fried Pickles

These fried pickles make an amazing snack. They do get soggy if left out for too long, so they are best enjoyed immediately. They are also better to eat when they are nice and warm. You can make a dip or enjoy them as is.

Time: 30 minutes

Servings: 5

Prep Time: 10 minutes

Cook Time: 20 minutes

Ingredients:

- Oil for frying
- ½ cup all-purpose flour
- 1 teaspoon Italian seasoning
- 1 ½ teaspoons garlic powder
- ¼ teaspoon salt
- ¼ teaspoon black pepper

- 1 tablespoon hot sauce
- ½ cup water
- 16 ounces dill pickles, sliced, drained and dried on paper towels

Directions:

1. Place a pot over medium to high heat and pour in about 1 to 2 inches of oil.
2. Take out a shallow bowl and whisk together the seasoning, garlic powder, flour, salt, and pepper. Add the hot sauce and water and mix until a smooth batter has formed.
3. Working in batches, place a few pickle slices into the batter and toss to coat.
4. Use a fork or a slotted spoon to remove the pickles from the batter and allow the excess to drop off into the bowl. Place the pickles into the oil, one at a time.
5. Fry for about 1 to 2 minutes or until they are golden brown.
6. Remove from the oil and place on paper towels to drain.
7. Once all of them have been fried, you can serve and enjoy.

✿ *Greek salad*

Greek salad is a classic. You can enjoy it as a main, or you can have it as a side. It is delicious, crispy, and an amazing way to use all the vegetables you have grown in your garden.

Time: 20 minutes

Servings: 4

Prep Time: 20 minutes

Cook Time: 0 minutes

Ingredients:

- 6 tablespoons of lemon juice, preferably freshly squeezed
- 2 cloves garlic, minced
- 2 teaspoons kosher salt, plus more to taste
- 1 cup extra-virgin olive oil
- 2 teaspoons minced fresh oregano
- Freshly ground black pepper
- 1 head romaine lettuce (about 1 pound), just the leaves, torn into bite-sized pieces
- 6 ounces kalamata olives
- ½ pound Feta cheese, crumbled
- 1 English cucumber, cut into 1 inch chunks

- 12 ounces vine-ripened cherry tomatoes, halved
- 1 small red onion, cut into ½ inch wedges, soaked in cold water for 5 minutes and drained
- 1 green pepper, seeded and diced

Directions:

1. To prepare your dressing, whisk together lemon juice, salt, garlic, and oil. Stir in the pepper and oregano to taste. Leave this to the side.
2. Take up a large bowl and toss the lettuce with some of the dressing. Divide into the serving bowls and scatter the rest of the ingredients equally amongst them.
3. Serve, and leave the rest of the dressing on the table for everybody to add extra to their own salad.

✿ *Green Peas and Potatoes*

This is a slightly spicy dish that is incredibly flavorful for something so simple. You can have it as a side dish or enjoy it with some flatbread or rice as a main dish.

Time: 30 minutes

Servings: 4

Prep Time: 5 minutes

Cook Time: 25 minutes

Ingredients:

- 3 cups of potatoes, cubed
- 1 green chili
- 2 tablespoons sunflower oil
- 1 teaspoon cumin seeds
- ½ teaspoon turmeric
- 1 teaspoon fresh ginger, grated
- ½ teaspoon salt
- 1 cup frozen peas
- ½ lemon
- Handful fresh coriander leaves

Directions:

1. Place a saucepan over high heat and add water. Peel the potatoes and, then chop them up add them to the boiling water. Add some salt and cover.
2. Allow the potatoes to cook for about ten to fifteen minutes and then drain.
3. Cut up the chili and put to the side.
4. Place a frying pan on the heat and add some oil to it.

5. Once the oil is hot add the cumin seeds and fry until they turn brown. Now add the chili, ginger, and turmeric.

6. Add in the potatoes and sprinkle over with some salt. Cover and cook for about five minutes.

7. Pull in the peas and stir. Cook for another five minutes until the potatoes are browning and tender. Remove from the heat.

8. Pour in the lemon juice and sprinkle with coriander.

9. Serve hot.

✿ Smoky Grilled Pizza With Greens and Tomatoes

Everybody loves a good pizza, and this one is a great way to add a ton of vegetables to it. If you do not want to make the pizza base from scratch, you can use a store-bought pizza base.

Time: 30 minutes

Servings: 2 pizzas

Prep Time: 15 minutes

Cook Time: 15 minutes

Ingredients:

Pizza Dough:

- 3 cups of all-purpose flour
- 2 teaspoons kosher salt
- 1 teaspoon active dry yeast
- 3 tablespoons olive oil, divided
- 1-¼ to 1-½ cups warm water (120° to 130°F)

Topping:

- 2 tablespoons olive oil
- 10 cups of beet greens, chopped
- 4 garlic cloves, minced
- 2 tablespoons balsamic vinegar
- ¾ cup prepared pesto
- ¾ cup shredded Italian cheese blend
- ½ cup crumbled feta cheese
- 2 medium heirloom tomatoes, thinly sliced
- ¼ cup fresh basil leaves, chopped

Directions:

1. You will start by making the pizza dough. Take out your food processor and add the flour, salt, and yeast. Pulse until everything has blended well.

2. Add 2 tablespoons of oil and water in a steady stream. Make sure that the food processor continues to work.

3. Once a dough ball has formed, you can turn out the dough onto a floured surface.

4. Knead the dough until you have a smooth and elastic consistency. It can take anywhere between 5 and 10 minutes. Make sure to flour your hands so that you do not get dough stuck to them.

5. Take out a bowl and grease it before placing the dough into it. Grease the top of the dough and then cover to let it rise for about one to two hours. You will know the dough is ready once it has almost doubled.

6. Punch the dough down and turn it out onto a floured surface. Cut the dough into two equal portions.

7. Roll into a ball, and then use a rolling pin to roll out the dough into a 10-inch circle.

8. Place each pizza base onto greased pieces of foil and brush with oil. Cover and allow to rest for a 10-minute period. Place your baking tray into the oven to heat up.

9. While the pizza bases are resting, you can get the toppings ready. Place a saucepan on the heat and add the beet greens. Cook until they're

tender, which takes three to five minutes. Then add the garlic and cook for another 30 seconds. Remove this from the heat and stir in the vinegar.

10. Remove the baking tray from the oven and lightly grease it. Then add your pizza bases onto the rack. Allow to grill in the oven at a medium heat until the bottoms are browned. That should take three to five minutes. Turn the bases over and cook on the other side for another two minutes.

11. Remove from under the grill and spread with pesto, add the beet greens, cheese, and tomato.

12. Place the pizzas under the grill and cook on medium heat until the cheese melts. It should only take about five minutes.

13. Pull them out of the oven and sprinkle with fresh basil

14. Cut each pizza into four pieces and serve.

✿ *Cajun Sirloin With Mushroom Leek Sauce*

Nothing goes down better than a well-cooked steak. This is a restaurant-quality dish that can be made in 30 minutes, and it is so delicious. It is filled with nutritious vegetables as well as protein.

Time: 30 minutes

Servings: 4

Prep Time: 10 minutes

Cook Time: 20 minutes

Ingredients:

- 1 beef top sirloin steak (1-¼ pounds)
- 2 tablespoons Cajun seasoning
- 2 tablespoons olive oil
- ½ pound sliced assorted fresh mushrooms
- 1 medium leek, halved and sliced
- 1 tablespoon butter
- 1 teaspoon minced garlic
- 1-½ cups dry red wine or reduced-sodium beef broth
- ¼ teaspoon pepper
- ⅛ teaspoon salt

Directions:

1. First, take the Cajun seasoning and rub it on the steak. Allow it to stand for five minutes to allow the flavors to absorb into the meat.
2. Take a large skillet or frying pan and place it over medium heat. Add some oil and once it is heated up, place the steak in the pan. Cook on

each side for about seven minutes or until the meat is done to your liking.

3. Remove from the heat and allow the steak to rest.

4. Add mushrooms, leek, and butter into the pan. Then add the garlic in and cook.

5. Pour in the wine and sprinkle pepper and salt. Stir so that you can loosen up the brown bits that are stuck to the pan.

6. Turn off the heat and bring it to a boil until the liquid has reduced itself into a sauce.

7. Slice the steak and serve with your sauce and vegetables.

✿ Southern Fried BLT

A BLT is a classic sandwich for a reason. It is something that everyone enjoys eating because it is crispy and flavorful. It is also really simple to make. If you have any leftover bacon, then you can use that in your sandwich.

Time: 30 minutes

Servings: 4

Prep Time: 15 minutes

Cook Time: 15 minutes

Ingredients:

- ½ cup cornmeal
- 3 tablespoons all-purpose flour
- Pepper, to taste
- 2 medium green tomatoes, sliced ¼ in. thick
- Oil for frying
- 8 slices whole wheat bread, toasted
- ½ cup mayonnaise
- 12 bacon strips, fried
- Iceberg lettuce leaves

Directions:

1. Take out a bowl and mix the flour, cornmeal, and pepper together. Then dip tomato slices in the mixture to coat.
2. Take out a large pan or skillet and place it over medium heat. Pour some oil into the pan so that it covers the bottom.
3. Once the oil is hot, place the tomato slices in it to fry. Fry for 2 to 3 minutes or until browned.
4. Remove from the pan and drain on paper towels.
5. Take the toasted bread and spread it with mayonnaise. Then layer with the bacon, tomatoes, and lettuce.

6. Cut and serve.

✿ Italian Style Veggie Wraps

A veggie wrap is a fantastic way to enjoy your vegetables. This is a crunchy and delicious wrap you can enjoy for lunch or dinner. Feel free to add whatever other vegetables or ingredients you want in this wrap to add some extra flavor.

Time: 25 minutes

Servings: 6

Prep Time: 20 minutes

Cook Time: 5 minutes

Ingredients:

- 1 small zucchini, chopped
- 1 cup cubed provolone cheese
- 1 cup cubed hard salami
- 1 cup chopped fresh broccoli
- 1 medium tomato, chopped
- 12 pimiento-stuffed olives, chopped
- 12 pitted olives, chopped
- 4 green onions, chopped
- ¼ cup prepared zesty Italian salad dressing
- 3 tablespoons hot pepper sandwich relish

- 1 tablespoon Catalina salad dressing
- 6 romaine lettuce leaves
- 6 whole wheat tortillas

Directions:

1. Take out a large bowl and combine all the ingredients except for the romaine lettuce leaves and tortillas.
2. Allow to stand for a few minutes so that the dressing imparts its flavor into the vegetables.
3. Place the tortilla on a flat surface, and then add the romaine lettuce leaf on top.
4. Spoon on the filling and then fold up the bottom and sides of the wrap.
5. If it is not staying in place then use a toothpick to secure it.
6. Cut in half and serve.

✿ Grilled Zucchini With Onions

This is a straightforward dish to make, and it makes a great side with whatever protein you choose to eat it with. The charring on it gives it some added flavor, and this is a great addition to any summer cookout.

Time: 20 minutes

Servings: 4

Prep Time: 10 minutes

Cook Time: 10 minutes

Ingredients:

- 6 small zucchini, halved lengthwise
- 4 teaspoons olive oil, divided
- 2 green onions, thinly sliced
- 2 tablespoons lemon juice
- ½ teaspoon salt
- ⅛ teaspoon crushed red pepper flakes

Directions:

1. Take out a grill pan and place it over medium heat.
2. Oil your zucchinis, then place them on the hot grill.
3. Grill the zucchinis covered for about 10 minutes. Make sure to turn at least once.
4. Once cooked through, remove from the heat and place them in a large bowl.
5. Add the lemon juice, salt, pepper, green onions, and the remaining oil. Toss to make sure everything is coated, and then serve.

✿ *Tequila Lime Shrimp Noodles*

Instead of using traditional noodles in this dish, we are going to be using something called zoodles. This is just a zucchini that has been spiralized so that it resembles noodles. It is much healthier, and you can get just as much flavor into these zucchini spirals. It is also an amazing way to get more vegetables into your meals.

Time: 30 minutes

Servings: 4

Prep Time: 20 minutes

Cook Time: 10 minutes

Ingredients:

- 3 tablespoons butter, divided
- 1 shallot, minced
- 2 garlic cloves, minced
- ¼ cup tequila
- 1-½ teaspoons grated lime zest
- 2 tablespoons lime juice
- 1 tablespoon olive oil
- 1 pound uncooked shrimp, peeled and deveined
- 2 medium zucchini, spiralized
- ½ teaspoon salt
- ¼ teaspoon pepper

- ¼ cup minced fresh parsley
- Additional grated lime zest

Directions:

1. Take out a large cast-iron skillet and heat over medium heat. Add two tablespoons of butter and allow to melt.
2. Add the garlic and shallots to the pan and fry for two minutes.
3. Remove the pan from the heat. Pull in the tequila, lime juice, and lime zest. Stir until combined.
4. Place the pan back on the heat and allow the liquid to reduce. That should only take two to three minutes.
5. Pour in the olive oil and remaining butter.
6. Add the shrimp and zucchini.
7. Add salt and pepper to taste and allow to cook until the shrimp has turned pink and is fully cooked through.
8. Remove from the heat and sprinkle over with parsley and lime zest.
9. Plate it up and serve.

✿ *Cod & Asparagus Bake*

This is a full meal that you can make in one dish. The recipe calls for Romano cheese, but if you do not have this, then you can use Parmesan or whatever cheese you would like.

Time: 30 minutes

Servings: 4

Prep Time: 10 minutes

Cook Time: 20 minutes

Ingredients:

- 4 cod filets, about 4 ounces each
- 1 pound fresh thin asparagus, trimmed
- 1 pint cherry tomatoes, halved
- 2 tablespoons lemon juice
- 1-½ teaspoons grated lemon zest
- ¼ cup grated Romano cheese

Directions:

1. Start by preheating your oven to 375°F.
2. Take out a baking dish that is big enough for your asparagus and cod.

3. Brush the baking dish with oil and place in the cod and asparagus. It is best to lay down the asparagus and then place the cod on top of it if there is not enough space for it to all lay flat in the dish.

4. Brush with a bit more olive oil and lemon juice. Sprinkle over the lemon zest.

5. Sprinkle over the cheese and place in the oven to bake.

6. Bake for about 12 minutes or until the fish starts becoming flaky. Be careful not to overcook your fish, otherwise, it will be dry.

7. Remove the baking dish from the oven and preheat the broiler.

8. Broil the cod and asparagus for about two to three minutes, or until the vegetables have slightly browned.

9. Remove from the broiler and allow to cool slightly before serving.

✿ Savory String Beans

When you have to cook a meal, it can be really difficult to find the right sides to go with whatever main you are making. These string beans are a tasty side to any dish because they are packed with flavor and so easy to make.

Time: 25 minutes

Servings: 2

Prep Time: 5 minutes

Cook Time: 20 minutes

Ingredients:

- 4 bacon strips
- 2 cups cut green beans, fresh or frozen
- 1 cup water
- ½ cup chopped onion
- 2 tablespoons fresh basil, minced
- 1 bay leaf
- ¼ teaspoon dill seed
- ¼ teaspoon garlic powder
- ⅛ to ¼ teaspoon salt
- ⅛ teaspoon pepper

Directions:

1. Take out a skillet or nonstick pan and put it over medium heat. Put the bacon in the pan and cook until crispy.
2. Crumble the bacon and set it aside for later.

3. Drain out the bacon fat except for 1 tablespoon that you will use to cook the rest of the ingredients with.

4. In the pan, add the beans, onion, seasonings, and water. Bring to a boil and cook until the beans are tender. This will take about 15 to 20 minutes.

5. Once the beans have cooked, you can drain out any of the excess liquid, if there is any. Discard the bay leaf and stir in the crumbled bacon.

6. Serve warm.

✿ Pork Banh Mi Wraps

A banh mi is a type of Asian sandwich packed with flavor and is a solid choice for lunch or dinner in the summer or spring. It is traditionally served on a type of baguette roll, but in this recipe, we are going to be using a wrap. You can feel free to switch out the wrap for any other kind of bread or roll if you wish.

Time: 30 minutes

Servings: 4

Prep Time: 15 minutes

Cook Time: 15 minutes

Ingredients:

- 4 boneless pork loin chops
- ¼ teaspoon pepper
- 1 tablespoon olive oil
- ½ cup sweet chili sauce, divided
- 2 tablespoons reduced-sodium soy sauce
- 1-¼ cups shredded lettuce
- 1 medium carrot, peeled and shredded
- 2 tablespoons rice vinegar
- 4 bread wraps
- ¼ cup reduced-fat mayonnaise
- 1 small cucumber, peeled and sliced into strips
- ¼ cup chopped fresh cilantro
- 2 green onions, chopped
- ½ jalapeno pepper, seeded and thinly sliced
- Sriracha chili sauce

Directions:

1. Sprinkle pork chops with salt and pepper. Rub in and set aside.
2. Take out a large skillet or pan and heat it over medium heat. Add some oil and once it is heated up, add the chops.
3. Cook for 2 to 3 minutes on each side or until the pork has cooked through.
4. In a bowl, combine ¼ cup of sweet chili sauce and soy sauce.

5. Pour this over your chops and reduce the heat to low. Cook until the sauce has thickened, which should take about two minutes.

6. Remove the pan from the heat.

7. In a bowl, combine the carrots, lettuce, and rice vinegar. Stir together and set to one side.

8. Once the pork has cooled down slightly, slice it into strips. Throw the strips back into the skillet so you can coat them with the sauce from the pan.

9. Take your wraps and lightly toast them, then spread them with mayonnaise.

10. Place the pork on the wraps and then cover with the lettuce mixture. Layer the cucumber, cilantro, jalapeño, and green onions.

11. Pour over the remaining sweet chili sauce and fold the wraps. Serve with Sriracha.

✿ Garden Vegetable Primavera

This is a pasta dish that you can make with all of your delicious and fresh vegetables. It allows the vegetables to shine through so that you can get the full experience and enjoy them for what they are.

Time: 30 minutes

Servings: 4

Prep Time: 20 minutes

Cook Time: 10 minutes

Ingredients:

- 8 ounces uncooked fettuccine
- 2 medium zucchini, coarsely chopped
- 1 medium carrot, sliced
- 1 teaspoon Italian seasoning
- ¼ teaspoon salt
- 1 tablespoon olive oil
- 1 cup grape tomatoes
- 2 garlic cloves, minced
- ½ cup reduced-sodium chicken broth
- ⅓ cup white wine
- ½ cup grated Parmesan cheese
- ¼ cup minced fresh basil

Directions:

1. Place a pot of water over high heat and allow it to boil. Add the fettuccine and cook according to the package instructions.
2. Take out a large pan or skillet and place it over medium heat with some oil. Add the zucchini, carrots, salt, and Italian seasoning and cook until the vegetables are firm but tender.

3. Add in the garlic and tomatoes and cook for another minute.
4. Pour in the wine and broth and stir to combine everything together.
5. Bring this to a boil and cook until the liquid has reduced by about half.
6. Drain your pasta and add it to the sauce. Add in the cheese and basil and toss.
7. Serve.

❀ Garden Pork Stir Fry

This is such an easy recipe that you can quickly whip together in the middle of the week. It is packed with flavor, and you can use many of your seasonal vegetables. Feel free to switch out the vegetables that are listed for things that you have in your garden.

Time: 30 minutes

Servings: 4

Prep Time: 15 minutes

Cook Time: 15 minutes

Ingredients:

- 1 pound boneless pork loin, cut into ¾ inch cubes

- 2 cups julienned zucchini
- ½ pound fresh mushrooms, sliced
- 1 medium onion, cut into wedges
- 1 cup julienned green pepper
- 1 tablespoon cornstarch
- 3 tablespoons reduced-sodium soy sauce
- 1 tablespoon cold water
- ¼ teaspoon garlic powder
- Cooked rice

Directions:

1. Take out a large skillet or pan and spray with some cooking spray.
2. Add this to a medium heat, and once it is hot, stir fry the pork until it has cooked through.
3. Add the onions, green pepper, mushrooms, and zucchini. Stir fry for another three minutes.
4. In a bowl, mix together the soy sauce, water, garlic powder, and cornstarch until you have a smooth consistency.
5. Pour this into the skillet and bring it to a boil. Allow to cook for about two minutes, and then serve your pork with some rice on the side.

✿ *Whole Grain Chowmein*

This is a different take on the traditional spaghetti and meatballs. It adds in a lot more vegetables and gives it some Asian flavors instead of the regular Italian flavors we are all used to. If you are getting bored of your regular pasta dishes then try this one out, because it is definitely going to be a hit even with the picky eaters in your family.

Time: 30 minutes

Servings: 4

Prep Time: 10 minutes

Cook Time: 20 minutes

Ingredients:

- 6 ounces uncooked whole-wheat spaghetti
- 2 tablespoons canola oil
- 2 cups small fresh broccoli florets
- 2 bunches baby bok choy, trimmed and cut into 1-inch pieces
- ¾ cup fresh baby carrots, halved diagonally
- ½ cup reduced-sodium chicken broth, divided
- 3 tablespoons reduced-sodium soy sauce, divided

- ¼ teaspoon pepper
- 4 green onions, diagonally sliced
- 2 tablespoons hoisin sauce
- 12 ounces refrigerated, fully cooked meatballs
- 1 cup bean sprouts
- Additional sliced green onions

Directions:

1. Set a pot of water to boil, and then add your pasta to cook according to the package directions. Once fully cooked, drain and set aside.
2. Take out a large nonstick pan or skillet and heat over medium heat.
3. Add the bok choy, broccoli, and carrots. Stir often for about four minutes.
4. Put in a ¼ cup of broth along with a tablespoon of soy sauce and pepper to taste.
5. Mix together and reduce the heat slightly. Allow to cook for about five minutes or until the vegetables are tender.
6. Stir the green onions into the mix, and then remove it from the heat.
7. Pour out the contents of the skillet and set it aside. Using the same skillet, stir together the

hoisin sauce with the remaining broth and soy sauce, then add the meatballs.

8. Cook for about five minutes or until everything has heated through.
9. Add the bean sprouts, broccoli mixture, and spaghetti into the skillet and heat through completely.
10. Serve and add additional green onions for garnish.

✿ Bruschetta Steak

This is a great dinner dish you can make when your vegetable garden has given you some amazing produce. It is delicious and full of flavor. Any steak lover will really enjoy this meal.

Time: 25 minutes

Servings: 4

Prep Time: 10 minutes

Cook Time: 15 minutes

Ingredients:

- 3 medium tomatoes, chopped
- 3 tablespoons minced fresh basil
- 3 tablespoons chopped fresh parsley

- 2 tablespoons olive oil, plus a little extra for the bread
- 1 teaspoon minced fresh oregano or ½ teaspoon dried oregano
- 1 garlic clove, minced
- ¾ teaspoon salt, divided
- 1 beef flat iron or top sirloin steak, cut into four portions
- ¼ teaspoon pepper
- Grated Parmesan cheese, optional
- 1 long bread roll, cut into slices

Directions:

1. Combine the tomatoes, basil, parsley, olive oil, oregano, and garlic clove. Sprinkle over a bit of salt and pepper and mix together. Set aside for later.
2. Take your bread slices and brush with olive oil. Sprinkle with salt, then place under the grill until golden brown and crispy.
3. Sprinkle steaks with salt and pepper.
4. Take a large skillet and grill your steak on medium heat for about 4 to 6 minutes on each side. Cook until your steak is done to your liking.

5. Remove the steak from the heat and allow it to rest for a few minutes before slicing and serving.

6. Add the tomato mixture on top of your steak and plate up with a few slices of crispy bread.

LEAVE A 1-CLICK REVIEW!

Customer reviews

★★★★★ 5 out of 5

1 global rating

5 star		100%
4 star		0%
3 star		0%
2 star		0%
1 star		0%

˅ How customer reviews and ratings work

Review this product

Share your thoughts with other customers

Write a customer review

I'd be incredibly grateful if you could take just 60 seconds to leave a review, even if it's just a few sentences!

Scan the QR Code Below to Leave a Quick Review!

CONCLUSION

Raised bed gardening is a very exciting journey and rewarding once you reap the literal fruit of your labor. You will definitely not get bored because there are so many different kinds of plants, fruits, and vegetables that you can grow throughout your gardening career. As you continue doing it, you will get better at it and find that the process gets a lot easier. It almost becomes muscle memory because you can start picking out diseases, picking out the fruits and vegetables that work best for you, and understanding your garden better as a whole.

Now that you have come to the end of this book, you have a good knowledge base to begin your journey. I suggest you go back to the beginning of the book and start planning and preparing. Think about the type of raised bed garden you want to build and what steps you need to take to do it. Start planning out a budget to know whether you have to save for it or can afford it right now. Going in with a plan will make everything much easier, and you'll have a better chance of getting precisely what you want. It can be really disappointing to start a project and then realize that you don't have what you need or you cannot afford it. Simply taking half an hour to properly think over exactly what you need is going to be so helpful.

Once you have done that, you can start researching materials for your raised bed garden. You mustn't just buy the first thing that you find. It is very much likely that you will find items for a much better price or much better quality if you just take some time to do research. Ask as many questions as possible and ensure that you are getting something that will stand the test of time. In most cases, your raised bed garden is something you will keep for a long time. You don't want to pick something that is extremely cheap just for the sake of it. This can end up biting you in the butt later on.

If this is your first raised bed garden, I would suggest just starting with one. Sometimes we can get excited and try to do too much at a time. Instead, start with one raised bed and ensure you understand how it works and the types of plants you will be growing in that raised bed garden. Once you are comfortable with the idea and know what to do, you can move on to growing your raised bed garden. Many people have multiple raised beds in their yards or properties. However, this can be a substantial financial commitment to put down all at once. This is why it is always better to start small and go from there. You will also be able to get into a routine and get used to taking care of plants. One raised bed garden will not be overwhelming, and you will fare a lot better with it.

Once you have started working on your raised bed garden, you will see how much joy comes from it. Gardening and taking care of your plants is a fun hobby, and it allows you to get outside and take care of something that is living. You will also be rewarded with fresh produce at the end of the growing season. This is probably one of the most rewarding aspects of having a raised bed garden. Even if you're not going to plant fruit and vegetables, just seeing your flowers blossom or the lush greenery start to show at the end of spring is definitely worth it.

At this point, you have all the tools that you need to get moving with your raised bed garden. Planning might not be the most exciting part of the process, but it is necessary. Start preparing now so that you will be ready to take action and plant when the growing season comes around. This is such an enjoyable journey, and I know you will find so much joy and satisfaction.

REFERENCES

Amy. (2022, April 20). *12 steps to preventing garden pests naturally*. Tenth Acre Farm. https://www.tenthacre farm.com/preventing-garden-pests/

BBC Gardeners' World Magazine. (n.d.). *How to grow vegetables – beginner veg to grow*. BBC Gardeners' World Magazine. https://www.gardenersworld.com/plants/ vegetable-crops-for-beginners/

Besemer, T. (2021, January 25). *14 common raised bed mistakes you must avoid*. Rural Sprout. https://www. ruralsprout.com/raised-bed-mistakes/

Bird netting installation guide. (n.d.). PestFix. https:// www.pestfix.co.uk/bird-netting-installation-guide.asp

Bruschetta steak. (n.d.). *Bruschetta steak*. Taste of Home. https://www.tasteofhome.com/recipes/bruschetta-steak/

Cajun sirloin with mushroom leek sauce. (n.d.-b). Taste of Home. https://www.tasteofhome.com/recipes/cajun-sirloin-with-mushroom-leek-sauce/

Cod and asparagus bake. (n.d.). Taste of Home. https://www.tasteofhome.com/recipes/cod-and-asparagus-bake/

Common pests and diseases. (n.d.). RHS. https://schoolgardening.rhs.org.uk/resources/info-sheet/common-pests-and-diseases

Crop rotations. (n.d.). Rodale Institute. https://rodaleinstitute.org/why-organic/organic-farming-practices/crop-rotations/#:~:text=Crop%20rotation%20is%20the%20practice

DeannaCat. (2021, February 5). *Choosing the best materials for raised garden beds*. Homestead and Chill. https://homesteadandchill.com/materials-raised-garden-beds/

Domoney, D. (2019, March 11). *Beginner's guide to growing fruit and veg*. David Domoney. https://www.

daviddomoney.com/beginners-guide-to-growing-fruit-and-veg/#:~:text=Good%20crops%20need%20good%20soil

Double digging. (n.d.). RHS Gardening. https://www.rhs.org.uk/soil-composts-mulches/double-digging

Drip irrigation system planning and installation guide. (n.d.). Easy Garden Irrigation. https://www.easygardenirrigation.co.uk/pages/drip-irrigation-system-planning-and-installation-guide

5 tips for improving your raised bed garden soil. (n.d.). Clean Air Gardening. https://www.cleanairgardening.com/5-tips-for-improving-your-raised-bed-garden-soil-2/

Food Network Kitchen. (2001). *Greek salad*. Food Network. https://www.foodnetwork.com/recipes/food-network-kitchen/greek-salad-recipe-2011681

Garden pork stir-fry. (n.d.). Taste of Home. https://www.tasteofhome.com/recipes/garden-pork-stir-fry/

Garden vegetable primavera. (n.d.). Taste of Home. https://www.tasteofhome.com/recipes/garden-vegetable-primavera/

Grant, A. (2021, March 25). *Garden layout plans – tips on layout options for the garden.* Gardening Know How. https://www.gardeningknowhow.com/edible/vegeta bles/vgen/layout-options-for-gardens.htm

Grant, B. L. (2022, April 12). *Seed starting times: When to start seeds for your garden.* Gardening Know How. https://www.gardeningknowhow.com/garden-how-to/propagation/seeds/when-to-start-seeds.htm

Grant, B. L. (2021, January 24). *Vegetable intercropping – information for interplanting flowers and vegetables.* Gardening Know How. https://www.gardening knowhow.com/edible/vegetables/vgen/vegetable-intercropping.htm

Griffiths, M. (2021, December 19). *Best fruit trees – 10 to grow in your backyard.* Homes and Gardens. https://www.homesandgardens.com/advice/best-fruit-trees

Grilled zucchini with onions. (n.d.). Taste of Home. https://www.tasteofhome.com/recipes/grilled-zucchini-with-onions/

How to do companion planting. (n.d.). Worcestershire Wildlife Trust. https://www.worcswildlifetrust.co.uk/actions/how-do-companion-planting?gclid=

CjOKCQjw0umSBhDrARIsAH7FCoftG3POZ3592X
OTc3CZ9QO_tq6R82Y2NrB_i0KQRj5HzSYdvIxb
QCEaAshtEALw_wcB

How to grow fruits and berries. (2021, January 28).
Gardener's Supply. https://www.gardeners.com/how-
to/growing-fruits-and-berries/5067.html

How to install drip irrigation. (n.d.). Instructables.
https://www.instructables.com/How-to-Install-Drip-
Irrigation/

How to water your plants. (n.d.). Longfield Gardens.
https://www.longfield-gardens.com/article/How-to-
Water-Your-Plants

Iannotti, M. (2021, July 27). *How to use succession
planting in your garden.* The Spruce. https://www.thes
pruce.com/succession-planting-1403366

Italian-style veggie wraps. (n.d.). Taste of Home.
https://www.tasteofhome.com/recipes/italian-style-
veggie-wraps/

Johnson, A. (2021, December 17). *Fried pickles recipe.*
She Wears Many Hats. https://shewearsmanyhats.com/
fried-pickles-recipe/

Julita. (2010, October 1). *Difference between seeds and seedlings.* Difference Between Similar Terms and Objects. http://www.differencebetween.net/science/ difference-between-seeds-and-seedlings/#:~:text=1

Kevin. (2022, May 11). *Raised bed herb garden: spicing things up.* Epic Gardening. https://www.epicgardening. com/raised-bed-herb-garden/#:~:text=Mediter ranean%20herbs%3A%20rosemary%2C% 20marjoram%2C

Lamp'l, Joe. (2018b, March 8). *Raised bed gardening, pt. 1: Getting started.* Joe Gardener. https://joegardener.com/ podcast/raised-bed-gardening-pt-1/#:~:text=Raised% 20beds%20provide%20you%20control

Living Lightly in Ireland. (n.d.). *Growing fruit and veg; design & layout 2022.* Living Lightly in Ireland. https:// livinglightlyinireland.com/2019/02/15/growing-fruit- and-veg-design-layout/

Miller, L. (2020, September 28). *Gardening with herbs – herb garden tips and tricks.* Gardening Know How. https://www.gardeningknowhow.com/edible/herbs/ hgen/herb-garden-tips-and-tricks.htm

Mulches and mulching. (n.d.). RHS. https://www.rhs.

org.uk/soil-composts-mulches/mulch

Nolan, T. (2017, April 4). *6 things to think about before preparing a raised bed garden*. Savvy Gardening. https://savvygardening.com/preparing-a-raised-bed-garden/#:~:text=Your%20raised%20bed%20could%20go

Noyes, A. (2022, April 24). *20 easiest vegetables to grow in raised garden beds or containers*. Gardening Chores. https://www.gardeningchores.com/easiest-vegetables-to-grow-in-raised-beds/

O'Neill, T. (2022, February 26). *How to stake a raised garden bed in 11 steps*. Simplify Gardening. https://simplifygardening.com/stake-a-raised-garden-bed/

Oblas, D., Schaeffer, Z., & Valeris, M. (2022, March 14). *Everything you need to know to build a simple raised bed*. Good Housekeeping. https://www.goodhousekeeping.com/home/gardening/g20706096/how-to-build-a-simple-raised-bed/

Painter, S. (2022, March 13). *Best soil for a raised bed vegetable garden*. LoveToKnow. https://garden.lovetoknow.com/vegetable-garden/best-soil-raised-bed-vegetable-garden#:~:text=Compost%20Nutrients

Pork banh mi wraps. (n.d.). Taste of Home. https://www.tasteofhome.com/recipes/pork-banh-mi-wraps/

Raised-bed gardening. (2007, January 8). University of Missouri Extension. https://www.ea.gr/ep/organic/SPECIALISED/raised%20beds%20gardening/G6985%20Raised-Bed%20Gardening,%20MU%20Extension.pdf

Raised beds. (n.d.). RHS Gardening. https://www.rhs.org.uk/garden-features/raised-beds

Randaci, A. (n.d.). *Common plant diseases & disease control for organic gardens.* Earth's Ally. https://earthsally.com/disease-control/common-plant-diseases.html

Reilly, K. (2022, April 18). *8 common raised garden mistakes you might be making.* Better Homes & Gardens. https://www.bhg.com/gardening/how-to-garden/raised-bed-garden-mistakes/

Savory string beans. (n.d.). Taste of Home. https://www.tasteofhome.com/recipes/savory-string-beans/

Smoky grilled pizza with greens & tomatoes. (n.d.). Taste of Home. https://www.tasteofhome.com/recipes/smoky-grilled-pizza-with-greens-tomatoes/

Southern fried BLT. (n.d.). Taste of Home. https://www.tasteofhome.com/recipes/southern-fried-blt/

Spicy potatoes and green peas. (2005, January). Delicious Magazine. https://www.deliciousmagazine.co.uk/recipes/spicy-potatoes-and-green-peas/

Tequila lime shrimp zoodles. (n.d.). Taste of Home. https://www.tasteofhome.com/recipes/tequila-lime-shrimp-zoodles/

The importance of pruning: Protect your plants and property. (2017, September 22). The Grounds Guys. https://www.groundsguys.com/blog/2017/september/the-importance-of-pruning-protect-your-plants-an/

Thompson, G., & Nair, A. (2021, May 10). *Yard and garden: Raised bed questions answered.* News. https://www.extension.iastate.edu/news/yard-and-garden-raised-bed-questions-answered

Tilley, N. (2022, February 17). *Recipes from the vegetable garden.* Gardening Know How. https://www.gardeningknowhow.com/edible/vegetables/vgen/recipes-from-the-vegetable-garden.htm

Tomato fritters. (n.d.). Taste of Home. https://www.tasteofhome.com/recipes/tomato-fritters/

Vanheems, B. (2016, February 12). *Choosing a location for your new vegetable beds*. GrowVeg. https://www.growveg.co.uk/guides/whats-the-best-position-for-your-vegetable-garden/

Walliser, J. (n.d.). *Plant diseases in the garden: How to prevent and control them*. Savvy Gardening. https://savvygardening.com/plant-diseases-in-the-garden-prevent-control/

What is the best soil for fruit trees? (2018, August 21). Spring Pot. https://www.springpot.com/best-soil-for-fruit-trees/#:~:text=In%20general%2C%20fruit%20trees%20thrive

What is irrigation? Types, methods and importance of irrigation. (n.d.). BYJUS. https://byjus.com/biology/irrigation/#drip-irrigation

When to plant vegetables: A guide to sowing and harvesting vegetables. (n.d.). Love the Garden. https://www.lovethegarden.com/uk-en/article/when-plant-vegetables-guide-sowing-and-harvesting-vegetables

Whole grain chow mein. (n.d.). Taste of Home.https://
www.tasteofhome.com/recipes/whole-grain-chow-
mein/

IMAGE REFERENCES

Braxmeier, H. (2012). Grape leaf smallpox mite [Image].
Pixabay. https://pixabay.com/photos/grape-leaf-small
pox-mite-infestation-56054/

Breen, D. (2015). Vegetables fruits food [Image].
Pixabay. https://pixabay.com/photos/vegetables-fruits-
food-ingredients-1085063/

Congerdesign (2016). Garden raised bed [Image].
Pixabay. https://pixabay.com/photos/garden-raised-
bed-bed-plants-1427541/

Conscious Design (2020). Person holding stainless steel
round tray with food [Image]. Unsplash. https://
unsplash.com/photos/3D43SBDDkAc

Farbsynthese (2020). Self-cultivation salad vegetable
[Image]. Pixabay. https://pixabay.com/photos/self-culti
vation-salad-vegetable-5345147/

Fox, A. (2020). Garden salad raised bed [Image]. Pixabay. https://pixabay.com/photos/garden-salad-raised-bed-nourishment-5223912/

Goellner, A. (2019). Raised bed chili chives [Image]. Pixabay. https://pixabay.com/photos/raised-bed-chili-chives-garden-4392783/

Grabowska, K. (2020). [Image]. Pexels. https://www.pexels.com/photo/close-up-photo-of-hose-watering-a-plant-4207906/

Green, P. (2016). Firewood lot [Image]. Unsplash. https://unsplash.com/photos/mGQfQe3EOBI

Gunaydin, N. (2014). Green metal garden shovel filled with brown soil [Image]. Unsplash. https://unsplash.com/photos/BduDcrySLKM

Hamersmit, A. (2019). Brown snail on green leaf [Image]. Unsplash. https://unsplash.com/photos/8oT2MA33jsk

H. M. (2020, October 17). Pink and yellow tulips field [Image]. Unsplash. https://unsplash.com/photos/78HoiJD0ClM

Ktryna. (2020). Herbs garden green [Image]. Pixabay. https://pixabay.com/photos/herbs-garden-green-nature-herb-5267073/

Mai, U (2015). Garden raised bed cabbage [Image]. https://pixabay.com/photos/garden-raised-bed-cabbage-gardening-883095/

Spiske, M. (2016). Selective focus photo of plant sprouts [Image]. Unsplash. https://unsplash.com/photos/vrbZVyX2k4I

Urban, F. (2021). Boy in black and white long sleeve shirt standing beside gray metal watering can during daytime [Image]. Unsplash. https://unsplash.com/photos/ffJ8Qa0VQU0

Valencia, M. (2014). Mustard food plant [Image]. Pixabay. https://pixabay.com/photos/mustard-food-plant-mustard-plant-248024/

Made in United States
Orlando, FL
20 August 2024

50585712R10100